20
THINGS
THAT
WOULD
MAKE
THE
NEWS
BETTER

20 THINGS THAT WOULD MAKE THE NEWS BETTER

ROGER MOSEY

Biteback Publishing

First published in Great Britain in 2022 by
Biteback Publishing Ltd, London
Copyright © Roger Mosey 2022

ISBN 978-1-78590-754-8

10 9 8 7 6 5 4 3 2 1

A CIP catalogue record for this book is available from the British Library.

Set in Minion and Trade Gothic

Printed and bound in Great Britain by
CPI Group (UK) Ltd, Croydon CR0 4YY

To Dorothy Farrell and in memory of Austin Mitchell. My first mentors in broadcasting and proud citizens of Yorkshire.

CONTENTS

PREFACE

This is a book about news and why it matters, in which you'll find plenty of hobby horses. A whole herd of them, if I'm honest, and I hope you will become fond of at least some.

It began in 2018 with an invitation from Selwyn College's development director Mike Nicholson to talk to alumni and friends about my years at BBC News, and we came up with the title '10 Things to Make the News Better'. The idea was to focus on the positive and to weld my experience in newsrooms during my thirty-three years at the BBC with the observations and prejudices of an enthusiastic consumer of broadcast news now living in Cambridge. It seemed to go down well, particularly in that my hobby horses were joined by lots of new ones. Members of the audience added a list of things they like and things they don't, though I had to tell them it really was no longer my responsibility that journalists don't understand the difference between 'less than' and 'fewer than'.

I then developed some of the themes further in the United States, through a lecture at the University of California in Los Angeles. The event was jointly arranged with Cambridge in America and BAFTA Los Angeles, and it had some American hobby horses to join the British ones. At the time, the coverage of Donald Trump was the thorniest of issues and it helped shape thoughts about the responsibilities of media organisations and their connection with the electorate. The audience in the UCLA lecture theatre had a spirited debate in the question-and-answer session about what to add to and subtract from the list of proposed improvements to news coverage.

So, now, following a kind invitation from my friends at Biteback Publishing, I'm taking this a stage further: updating the thoughts – doubling the size of the herd – and inviting a new audience to join the discussion. And there are some ground rules I need to explain. First, this is overwhelmingly about broadcast news – partly because it's what I know about, but also because it is still central to national and international debates. Second, it will talk about the BBC more than any other organisation – again, because it's something I'm familiar with and because it does actually matter more than most. It should be, and often is, the gold standard. I particularly salute its staff, who work tirelessly to do the best they can despite the geographical relocations and internal reorganisations which drive them up the wall. Third, it will dwell quite a lot on politics, because the relationship between Westminster and the media is broken and needs the most attention. By contrast, foreign reporting – delivered by some outstanding correspondents – is going through a conspicuously strong phase, as we've seen most recently in Ukraine and in revelatory broadcasts from Afghanistan, Yemen, Ethiopia and even America, where ITV's coverage of the 6 January 2021 Capitol insurrection deservedly won awards galore. And fourth, I absolutely do not believe in the myth of a golden age. There were many bad things in the past, just as there are some areas that should be improved today. My contention is that it should be possible to merge the best of then with the best of now.

In the past, some BBC managers have become grumpy about dinosaurs like me critiquing their organisation. Well, I love it too, but it belongs to all of us and I believe it's right for there to be accountability for the BBC's practices and policies. If it's to be one of the most open organisations in Britain, which it has struggled to achieve in the past, then it needs challenge and analysis. There is plenty of space between those who argue that the BBC can do no wrong and the folk who want to destroy it. In the term 'critical friend', both words matter, and I am unequivocal that I want the BBC to survive and thrive. Crucially, it can do that most effectively if it is at the top of its game. Recognising weaknesses is a part of that drive for excellence – because even with its faults it's a dozen times better than the unregulated and user-generated alternatives.

Yet the BBC is far from being the sole guarantor of standards in journalism. Every day I see and hear and read excellent journalism – from LBC radio to *The Times*, and from Sky News to *The Spectator* and *New Statesman*. Podcasts bring in new voices; social media allows the audience to answer back. There are so many sources of information and so much to enjoy.

But the warning signs are there too. These are fractured, difficult times. Media can spread hatred. Trust in authorities and in established media organisations is precarious, not least because the newer platforms, notably Twitter, can whip up a mob against them. So, it would be foolish to imagine that we can continue exactly as we are, and that's why we need to have the argument: how is it that we can make the news better – more relevant, more valuable, more ambitious – and through that try to bring our society closer together? What follows are thoughts and provocations to feed into the debate, and ultimately it will be the consumers of news who deliver their verdict. They will either stay with the mainstream media and encourage its reinvigoration or ensure its splintering into thousands of disparate pieces. And the stakes are so high because once it has fractured, there will be no putting it back together again.

CHAPTER 1

CHERISH PUBLIC SERVICE

My love affair with broadcast news began by night at my home in Bradford in the early 1970s. School work done, I would switch on a cheap transistor radio next to my bed and listen to *The World Tonight* – then one of Radio 4's newest programmes – and its main presenter Douglas Stuart. As now, this was a time of tumult. I learned about the Middle East oil crisis, the superpower tensions of the Cold War, the blood spilt on the streets of Northern Ireland; the world was brought directly to me through on-the-ground reporting and the painting of word pictures. The interviews with leading figures of the day were conducted courteously – the tougher stuff was left to Robin Day on television – and accompanied by analysis of what the latest developments meant for us all. If it was possible to feel calm amid the turbulence, I did: there was authority in the voices I heard, and this was not a programme where guests were booked to provide a punch-up. It was much more about enlightenment.

Even if you disagreed with what was being said, there was no recourse other than to write a letter to the BBC and receive the blandest of replies a week later from its audience services team. Douglas Stuart had the blessing of never trending on Twitter.

A little later in the Radio 4 schedule was another favourite for a politics-obsessed schoolboy: the nightly broadcast of *Today in Parliament*. In those days the programme relayed no braying of MPs or shouting down of party leaders, because it was still some years before the microphones were allowed into the parliamentary chambers and even longer until the arrival of television cameras. So, the passionate debates of the '70s – when Britain was considering whether to join the European Community – were rendered in the beautifully modulated tones of Radio 4 continuity announcers. Even so, the heat of the argument was unmistakable, with the Heath government under attack from its own Eurosceptics and the Labour Party also split and fighting a tactical war in the House of Commons. Armed with what I had learned from the nightly digests, as a sixteen-year-old I canvassed in the two 1974 general elections on behalf of the Liberal Party and earnestly told voters in Bradford South why I believed the two-party system had failed.

It wasn't only about radio. Live television via satellite had come of age for the first successful mission to the moon in 1969. Then, as a teenager, long after my parents had gone to bed, I would sit late into the night watching the Watergate hearings. The investigation into President Nixon's wrongdoings was an early example of extended rolling news coverage from abroad. The big days – when Nixon's aides John Ehrlichman and Bob Haldeman appeared before the congressional committee and faced the questioning of Senator Sam Ervin – saw a presidency being destroyed on our screens. The scheduling, right until the moment when we watched live as a helicopter flew a disgraced Nixon away from the White House, meant that this was history in which we could all share.

It is what public service broadcasting did, and still does. Spool forward fifty years and so much has changed: the proliferation of channels and platforms, the explosion of social media, the revolution in technology. But there are still plenty of places where experienced reporters and producers try to make sense of what's happening. The mission of the BBC and of other public service broadcasters (PSBs) in Britain and overseas – to create better-informed societies and to safeguard democracy – is essentially the same.

Crucially, that brings a duty to try to spread those values of tolerant, evidence-based discussion across the world. The fight for truth is difficult enough in liberal democracies, but it is tougher still when states intervene to wilfully distort the facts and to censor news they find inconvenient. When Ukraine was invaded in February 2022, the Russian disinformation campaign ramped up too. Jane Lytvynenko, research fellow at Harvard's Shorenstein Center on Media,

Politics and Public Policy, told NBC: 'We're going to see a huge onslaught, and we need to be prepared for that.' The responsibility of democratic broadcasters to stand by the truth grows ever greater, and Britain still has immeasurable soft power from its global information services.

So, Western broadcasters can define themselves against the malign state players, and they can also differentiate themselves from what wholly commercial organisations do. It is still hard to beat the crassness of the comments made by chief executive of the American CBS network Leslie Moonves during the rise of Donald Trump in the 2016 presidential campaign:

> It may not be good for America, but it's damn good for CBS ... Man, who would have expected the ride we're all having right now? ... The money's rolling in and this is fun ... I've never seen anything like this, and this is going to be a very good year for us. Sorry. It's a terrible thing to say. But, bring it on, Donald. Keep going.

The Facebook whistleblower Frances Haugen identified the same issue in that giant of social media: 'The thing I saw at Facebook over and over again was there were conflicts of interest between what was good for the public and what was good for Facebook. And Facebook, over and over again, chose to optimize for its own interests, like making more money.'

There are some cracks now appearing in the organisation, but a former senior executive at Facebook was scathing about its effects on us all: 'The short-term, dopamine-driven feedback loops that we have created are destroying how society works. No civil discourse, no co-operation; misinformation, mistruth.'

Put it together and it is frightening. Grotesque lies by states. Deliberate campaigns of propaganda and misinformation. Amplification by social media and the ill will of individuals. No matter what its most frothing and deranged critics would say, the BBC never goes within a million miles of that – and it is, instead, a barrier against the onslaught of the bad actors. The first stated public purpose in the BBC's 2016 Charter is admirably clear:

> To provide impartial news and information to help people understand and engage with the world around them: the BBC should provide duly accurate and impartial news, current affairs and factual programming to build people's understanding of all parts of the United Kingdom and of the wider world. Its content should be provided to the highest editorial standards. It should offer a range and depth of analysis and content not widely available from other United Kingdom news providers, using the highest calibre presenters and journalists, and championing freedom of expression, so that all audiences can engage fully with major local, regional, national, United Kingdom and

global issues and participate in the democratic process, at all levels, as active and informed citizens.

These really are stretching targets. The BBC is promising not just a news service but excellent content at every level of its operations that other UK news providers are not supplying, and it is reasonable to judge it by the standards it has signed up to.

The wider aim of public service broadcasting has become trickier to define in an age of digital plenty. The Commons Digital, Culture, Media and Sport Committee said in 2021: 'It means different things to different people. To some it's their main source of current affairs and news, to others, it's sitting down together to watch *Strictly Come Dancing* on a Saturday night.' The MPs went on to try a better shot at its key characteristics:

First, universality of access is widely considered to be an integral part of public service broadcasting. It is expected that public service content is made widely available to all citizens of the UK, free at the point at which they consume it. There is also an expectation that this universally available content represents the diversity of the UK, and spans a wide range of genres to reflect that diversity. Secondly, it is expected that the news and current affairs content produced by PSBs be accurate, reliable and impartial. In short: consumers expect PSBs to be a trusted source of information. Finally, it is expected that PSBs should be able to function free from government interference or political pressure.

We should salute the MPs' triumph of hope over reality about government interference, but it's noteworthy how news is always at the top, or near the top, of any list of public broadcasting's key characteristics. There is a decent argument that news matters now even more than it did in the past because of the turbulence in the world and the threats to our democracies. Opponents of public service broadcasting argue that the market can do what the BBC and the likes of Channel 4 do, and they have at least half a point about drama and entertainment. Back in my 1970s Bradford home, the only television drama came from the BBC and ITV – and much of it was pretty good, bringing audiences of millions to classics and new writing alike. The public broadcasters are still in the game, but drama is an area where the American giants and international streaming services excel. I am one of many who believe that HBO's *Succession*, shown in the UK by Sky Atlantic, was one of the best dramas of recent years. And a former colleague who had top jobs at the BBC reckons there was a watershed moment during the 2010s, when *The Crown* was commissioned by Netflix: 'At that point the BBC could no longer say that it was the place for the very best high-end British drama.' Viewers have flocked to the newer platforms. Even allowing for Netflix's hype and inflated audience figures, *Bridgerton* – which is filmed here – and *Squid Game* were enormous successes in Britain.

The secondary argument was that the BBC was a guarantor of British-based content and media expertise, but even that has become shakier as the streamers have expanded their operations. Billions of pounds are being invested in studios and UK-based production. *Game of Thrones* was shot in Northern Ireland, and *The Lord of the Rings* has been relocated by Amazon from New Zealand to England, bringing hundreds of millions of dollars of investment. There is a studio boom across the home counties, and the streamers' content budgets now dwarf those of the BBC and ITV. So 'British content'? Well, not entirely: the blockbusters are targeted at international markets, and Britishness is a by-product rather than the essential mission of the BBC and a state-owned Channel 4. But smaller-scale British productions are now emanating from the streamers – think of *After Life* by Ricky Gervais – and the competition for the traditional broadcasters in drama and comedy is becoming more acute.

That may explain a question which Tim Davie, the director-general (DG) of the BBC since 2020, is fond of putting to opinion formers: 'Which show was the most popular on TV last night?' The answer on many days now is, surprisingly to many, the 6.30 p.m. regional news slot on BBC One – which exceeds the linear television audiences for *EastEnders* and network 'hit' comedies. Just before Christmas 2021, ITV's supposed blockbuster *I'm a Celebrity Get Me Out of Here* was watched by an audience of 4.6 million, while the BBC regional news scored 4.9 million. Each night it follows the highly successful *BBC News at Six*, which regularly gets some editions into each week's top twenty programmes across all channels, where it is joined among the most popular network shows by the *BBC News at Ten* and the *ITV Evening News*. In the first week of March 2022, when the war in Ukraine was dominating the headlines, the *News at Six* occupied five of the top six places in the weekly *Broadcast* network ratings chart, with only *Ant & Dec's Saturday Night Takeaway* preventing a clean sweep. Schedulers used to see the news bulletins as a drag on their performance – the channel commissioners' eyes would roll if we suggested extending a bulletin – whereas now they are among their top performers. It is wonderful, and an example of the power of live news, that ITV has decided to ride this tide by extending its evening bulletin to a full hour, thus putting more news into its peak schedule than the BBC.

The definitive research by the regulators at Ofcom confirms that television remains the most common platform for news among the British public, with 75 per cent of the population saying it's the place they usually go to for their news. There has been some decline in recent years, but nothing like the way that printed newspapers' circulations have fallen off a cliff. There is, however, a massive age differential for television news, with more than 90 per cent of the over-65s describing themselves as regular viewers, falling to 49 per cent for the 16–24 age group. But the main broadcast news providers in the United Kingdom are trusted. Sky News leads the way, seen as accurate (76 per cent) and trustworthy (74 per cent). The BBC and ITV are locked together around a decent 70 per cent on each indicator. This compares with lower levels of trust for the printed press and especially for user-generated content on social media, thus confirming that the British public retain their common sense.

The appetite for impartial news is still voracious. A 2022 BBC survey asked respondents to think about news generally and decide which was more important to them personally: news coverage that is impartial, or news coverage that reflects your point of view. Impartiality won by a landslide 87 per cent to 13 per cent, and even among younger viewers the margin was 76 per cent to 24 per cent.

It is inevitable that the fragmentation of audiences, and the always-on digital culture, affects news as it does other genres. We check our phones when we have a spare moment to keep across the latest developments, and the algorithms on Facebook and Twitter chirp away with the 'news for you' they have decided we should see. Often, though, this is news from the major providers. The likes of CNN, the *Washington Post* and all the public broadcasters have inserted themselves well into the digital space, and they remain anchors in a sea of rumour and disinformation. Social media amplifies the main bulletins: a little over 3 million people were watching the *ITV Evening News* when it broke the story of Allegra

Stratton's briefing on the Downing Street Christmas party that never was, but that clip – branded as an 'ITV exclusive' – was watched by more than 9 million within the following twenty-four hours.

Conventional scheduled news programmes remain live events amid the multitude of catch-up services – and when big moments happen, that is where we congregate. An astonishing 27 million people watched the UK Prime Minister Boris Johnson announce the start of the first lockdown, with 15 million on BBC One alone, which are figures never seen outside World Cup finals and the Olympic Games. Throughout the pandemic, conventional television news viewing surged – even though many of us had endless hours to fill surfing the internet, and there was often little fresh to hear by the time we got to ten at night. News remains the genre in which the BBC is a global leader through the BBC World Service.

Not everyone agrees with this emphasis on news, of course. The playwright Sir David Hare contributed an enjoyably disputatious piece to *The Guardian* in October 2021, which castigated the corporation for distorting its original aims, set out by Lord Reith in the 1920s, to 'inform, educate and entertain'. 'When [director-general John] Birt chose to pitch the BBC as the greatest news-gathering organisation in the world', writes Hare,

he caused nothing but problems. First, he narrowed the

far larger role the BBC was there to play. Second, he encouraged people to start asking why we needed the BBC at all. If its principal purpose was to gather news, there were a whole host of commercial outlets that could do the job just as well.

(We wait for Netflix News or Amazon Prime's version of *Look North* from Leeds.)

Hare ploughed on: 'If you doubt that news is thought to be the primary business, you will find it architecturally expressed if you visit Broadcasting House. Every other department is flattened against the walls of an overblown newsroom that draws all energy to the centre.'

Playwrights understandably want more plays. Journalists want more news. But of the three parts of the BBC mission, while 'inform' and 'educate' are still potentially distinctive (a revival of the BBC's education programming was one of the few upsides of the pandemic), it is 'entertain' which is now the most challenging. The previously ratings-winning Gordon Ramsay is one unlucky example of the phenomenon. His game show *Bank Balance* was a high-profile commission by the BBC to occupy the prime 9 p.m. slot on a number of nights in early 2021, but it plummeted in the ratings and went from boom to bust in being cancelled after one series. He re-emerged with *Future Food Stars*, which suffered the indignity of falling out of the Top 100 programmes, while other would-be entertaining occupants of the 9 p.m. slot – Wim Hof and Alan Carr – limped along with linear audiences of around 2 million.

Hare is also at odds with BBC bosses from multiple backgrounds who gathered at meetings in the early part of this century for contingency exercises concerning how the corporation might react to significant cost-cutting. I remember one session in a cheerless conference centre in Manchester, where we debated, if we had to cut and cut again, what would we preserve at all costs? The answer was BBC One, with its range of genres for a mass audience – and with an emphasis on well-resourced news bulletins as the daily landmarks of its schedule. Many said they would strive to keep the BBC News channel too. In radio, our last service standing would be Radio 4, with *Today* as its most important programme.

Inconveniently for Hare's argument, many long-standing commercial outlets have slashed their newsrooms. When I started work for the independent station Pennine Radio in Bradford in the late 1970s, we had eight newsroom journalists and there was a nightly hour-long digest of developments from across West Yorkshire. Try finding that now on your 'local' version of Heart or Magic FM. It was a similar story at ITV. The regions have become bigger and less local, and the staffing has become thinner. As for local newspapers, many have given up the ghost in print and have moved online, where a heritage of journalism valiantly battles with their owners' desire for clickbait. The tectonic plates of the digital media revolution are still in motion. In a year,

Facebook and Netflix lost hundreds of billions of dollars of value when consumer numbers began to fall. Twitter, the platform where online abuse is a way of life, is at the time of writing being toyed with by a billionaire whom we might kindly call 'eccentric'.

That is why well-funded public broadcasting is essential. Most of us would truly miss it if it wasn't there: no platform where the nation comes together for big events such as the Olympics or the World Cup or a *Strictly Come Dancing* final. None of those programmes you feel you own: the eccentric take on life squirreled away on BBC Four, or the talks on Radio 4 transporting you for fifteen minutes away from the hurly-burly. But sadly, this kind of output is under attack across the world. PBS in America and ABC in Australia have lost too many battles with unsympathetic governments.

I spent some time in my last years at the BBC on the board of the European Broadcasting Union (EBU), where, generally, there is a healthier picture, both in the UK and across Europe. But whenever directors-general and other senior executives gathered, the talk was about the battle to preserve funding in the face of the juggernauts of competition heading towards the legacy broadcasters. The European Union was seen as liberal economically and unsympathetic to state organisations, and many national governments only liked broadcasters they could influence and control. We recognised that innovation was needed, and Germany showed one possible way forward with its introduction of a household levy rather than the old-style licence fee. But ultimately, it's about money, and whether you have it or not. A report by the Reuters Institute for the Study of Journalism at Oxford sums it up:

> Comparative research looking at different cases across Europe suggests that public service media tend to have wider reach with their news in cases where they, like the BBC, are relatively well-funded, integrated, and centrally organized, and have a degree of strategic autonomy and insulation from direct political influence and greater certainty through multi-year agreements on public service remit, funding, and governance.

There was a golden period in which the Blair government, elected in 1997, was financially generous towards the BBC. Indeed, by 2002 it was said to be 'basking in a jacuzzi of spare public cash' by one of its rivals, the chief executive of Channel 4. That officeholder was Mark Thompson, who two years later became director-general of the BBC and promptly had to try to deny that it was true. But when Thompson appointed me as director of sport in 2005, there was manifestly no shortage of money. In my initial briefing within the division, I was told that we had enough in the budget to bid for live Premier League football, and we did just that; for a couple of years we could contemplate an expansion of our portfolio after years of decline. But then the financial weather began to change. Thompson removed tens of millions of pounds from the sport coffers, and by 2010 we were facing a Tory–Lib Dem administration dedicated to austerity. The licence fee was frozen by George Osborne as Chancellor.

BBC finances are opaque, and it is difficult to tell how authentically the corporation is crying the poor tale. Even as a member of the management team in 2010, I had thought a freeze would be disastrous – but we were told on the quiet that it would be OK really. Then, after I left, the BBC did a complex second deal with Osborne which gave it some inflation-based increases but also lumbered it with taking on the financing of licence fees for the over-75s. Initially, the BBC said this was all perfectly fine, but then it changed its tune and said it was facing a financial crisis and had no choice other than to withdraw the majority of free licences for the elderly. There are certainly ups and downs in the budget. One of the benefits for the BBC in recent years was the growth in the total number of licence fee-payers, which mitigated the miserly increases in the fee itself; and it also got a nice dollop of cash from the Foreign Office for its overseas services. However, further years of freeze – and with inflation running riot – cannot avoid taking their toll.

A National Audit Office report towards the end of 2021 confirmed that the BBC was on track to make savings totalling £1 billion because of the squeeze on its finances, with the consequences particularly apparent in BBC News. There were more than 1,800 redundancies across the corporation between the 2017/18 and 2020/21 financial years – and more than a fifth of those, 385 jobs, involved frontline journalists. Yet the amount of news output increased, partly because of the pandemic putting more of a premium on live and breaking coverage. It is little surprise that the auditor then notes: 'BBC surveys show that staff engagement in the news division has been lower than for the BBC as a whole over recent years.' Sorting this out will be a Herculean task for the new director of BBC News Deborah Turness, who was lured from ITV and has an impressive CV including a stint at NBC in the United States. It is unlikely to be possible unless the pressure for further cuts is eased.

Yet the political attacks on the corporation have sharpened. In early 2020, the *Sunday Times* reported the comments of a Downing Street adviser who opined that it was time to 'whack' the BBC and think about abolishing the licence fee and selling off many of its services. The rhetoric miraculously softened after Dominic Cummings had stopped being a Downing Street adviser, but there is still no love lost between SW1 and W1A. The appointment of Nadine Dorries as Culture Secretary was evidence of that, with one Westminster insider describing an introductory meeting with her as one of the most 'awful' he'd experienced as a media specialist. Sources close to Dorries used incidents that the government found displeasing, such as *Today* presenter Nick Robinson's prickly interview with Boris Johnson, to threaten future licence fee settlements. 'Nick Robinson has cost the BBC a lot of money' was one of the headlines inspired by a Culture Department briefing – which is a ludicrous way of deciding the proper level of funding for public broadcasting. The settlement, when it emerged, was tough, and accompanied by threats from Dorries that this would be the last ever deal involving a licence fee.

The government white paper on broadcasting published in spring 2022 was by no means all bad. For instance, it had sensible measures to keep major sporting events on free-to-air channels. But the recklessness in the government's approach is unmistakable. The Tory right looks longingly at the streaming companies and their subscription model – at precisely the time when Netflix is in the spotlight as a subscriber-losing, mega-debt-ridden American construct which many critics believe has lost its touch in commissioning. Scrapping the BBC licence fee, without having defined an alternative funding model, is a thoroughly un-conservative approach. If you already have a world-renowned broadcaster, why not invest in it? Starving the BBC of resources inhibits, rather than enables, the reforms the corporation needs. Similarly, the proposed privatisation of Channel 4 was portrayed as giving it the power to compete with Netflix, when at its best the channel is precisely the opposite of the streaming giants: quirky, distinctive, British – and transmitting programmes that nobody else would.

It would be an act of madness if we as a country threatened the existence of BBC News and *Channel 4 News*.

Former director of the Downing Street Policy Unit Geoff Mulgan put it at its starkest in the *New Statesman* in 2021: 'We are in a war for truth. The battle for truth is so fundamental that it has to precede any other priority.'

And ITV's political editor Robert Peston gave the wider context in his Hugh Cudlipp lecture in 2020:

> Global system breakdown has defined all our lives ... from the banking system's boom and bust, to the rise of a new anti-globalisation and populist generation of politician and political leader, to the mounting cost of global warming, to the exponentially charged proliferation of a jumping-the-species virus ... And we have a choice, as people, as nations, as culture. We can try to understand what's happening in a balanced, calm, rational, scientific way. And rebuild some sense of control over our destiny. Or we can continue shouting at each other in social media's Tower of Babel and turn *Call of Duty 4: Modern Warfare* into the model of our future. Or to put it another way, journalism we can trust, impartial journalism, matters more than it ever has, so that as citizens we have the information that allows us to make those reasoned choices.

Indeed. Although so much has changed, many millions of us still like the kind of voices I heard crackling through a Yorkshire night fifty or more years ago – the calm and professional within well-edited programming which tells us what has happened without hype and spin. Modernisation is right, too. But independent journalism needs fighting for more than ever, and we would all be poorer if the public broadcasters were to lose the war.

CHAPTER 2

COVER WHAT MATTERS

The biggest question about public broadcasting is a simple one: what does it give you that the market can't? And that applies even more acutely to news when we are assailed by it at every point of our day. So, let me try for the easiest possible formulation. Public service is best defined by covering the stories and issues that really matter and discarding the ones that don't.

Why this matters particularly in broadcast news is that programmes are really rather short. We used to calculate that if all the words spoken on the *BBC News at Ten* or *ITV Evening News* were printed on the front page of a broadsheet newspaper, there would still be some blank space – with the dozens of other pages completely empty. It has therefore always been an error to see a bulletin as being the equivalent of an entire newspaper, with headlines but also features and opinion and culture and sport. There must be some opportunity for what a wise old producer called 'light and shade' – some contrast between the stories, an opportunity to change the mood. But the purpose of a news bulletin is to share what we really must know about the events of the day and the impact they will have on our lives.

I am therefore unabashedly in favour of serious broadcast news. Websites and social media and magazines can entertain us, and we can enjoy memes and jokes and pictures of cuddly animals on a multitude of digital platforms. There is a 'free' or commercial model that can deliver all that. Of course, the infinite capacity of the internet means that established broadcasters can widen their agenda there too, and everyone should be allowed their bit of fun. But the core mission of public service broadcasting – shared, thankfully, by the people who run ITV and Sky and Channels 4 and 5 – should be to inform in a way that is explicitly different from the unregulated and unsubstantiated territory that is occupied by others.

Former director of BBC News Richard Sambrook put it simply in a recent exchange:

It's essential public broadcasters distinguish themselves from the rest of the market through the sheer quality of what they offer. In news that is most obviously done with a wider range of coverage – through primary newsgathering – and greater depth of analysis. Audiences need to know they can rely on PSBs for accurate, trustworthy, insightful news.

You can get immersed in the self-regarding stuff about news being the first draft of history, but the test is whether news organisations prepare their audiences for the stories that matter and help their understanding of a changing world. Over the decades, they have been strong on the end of the Cold War – but less so on the consequences that followed, as we are now witnessing. The Northern Ireland peace process was well covered, while the potential impact of Brexit on a fragile post-conflict society was ignored until it was too late. Middle East? Not bad. China? Not good enough. And my generation was slow in getting to grips with the technology revolution and what it brought with it, such as cyber attacks and cryptocurrencies, whose reverberations will intensify with time.

For the most part, standing on the higher ground works. Nobody could complain about the volume and seriousness of the PSBs' coronavirus coverage, or about their commitment to reporting from the world's zones of conflict. But there is always an itch to engage – key word – with different audiences and to bring light consumers of news into the flagship programmes. You can spot it a mile off. At one point while I was writing this book, I became irritated by the sheer amount of airtime devoted to the court case about Britney Spears's conservatorship. It was, of course, completely reportable: it should have been mentioned in the bulletins. But not with the prominence and at the length it was when there was so much else to cover, from Ukraine to climate change. There should be more restraint, too, on the advertorials about *Strictly Come Dancing* that worm their way into BBC news programmes. Beware any news item which concludes: 'And you can see that programme tonight on [name of channel] at 9 p.m.' It's either news or it's not, and bulletins are not marketing opportunities.

There is nothing new in this kind of debate. Decades ago, John Birt – when he was appointed to the BBC as deputy director-general and in charge of news in 1987 – told his executives that 'increasing the "authority" of BBC news was an absolute financial priority. That was what the licence fee was for.' According to the fabulously entertaining book *Fuzzy Monsters* by Chris Horrie and Steve Clarke, he is said to have added that 'reporters and editors needed to select items on the basis of their significance to the nation'. Birt's reforms demonstrably had an effect. The revamped *Nine O'Clock News* in particular was a vehicle for some highly ambitious examinations of the issues of its time, with an especially memorable episode which was presented from Moscow and gave lengthy explanations of exactly what 'glasnost' and 'perestroika' meant as the Soviet Union started to crumble.

You would probably not find a channel controller swooning with delight if you told them it was 'perestroika night on the news', but this was in line with the original mission of the BBC, which was a profoundly democratic one. Its first director-general, John Reith, saw its purpose as being 'that all and sundry, without let or hindrance, might enjoy the interests and diversions hitherto reserved for those with the twin keys of fortune – leisure and money'. He identified, too, the dilemma that has existed throughout the BBC's 100 years:

> In earliest years accused of setting out to give the public not what it wanted but what the BBC thought it should have, the answer was that few knew what they wanted, fewer what they needed. In any event, it was better to overestimate than to underestimate. If another policy had been adopted – that of the lowest common denominator – what then?

We should be thankful that Lord Reith did not live to see a recent BBC One Saturday night schedule with four celebrity game shows, one after another. I am guessing that he would not fancy a ride on Michael McIntyre's wheel. A stronger sense of Reith's mission persists in the corporation's news output, and many of the major stories are covered well – but it is at risk of being chipped away. Particularly insidious are the charts on news websites showing which the most popular stories are. Outside of major crises, they tend to be the wackier items, and there is no harm in that. But that should not influence the journalistic selection of stories for flagship bulletins and the way they are presented. My former boss

Helen Boaden, who spent many years as director of BBC News, spelt it out in her farewell address when she left the corporation. 'On the internet', she said,

> so-called 'clickbait' is often dangled to hook a reader in: broadly that means content of a sensational or provocative nature, to draw visitors to a particular web page ... Has this changed the journalistic zeitgeist for everyone? Does the new form of competition now lead, more often than it should, to the headline that is overwritten on more obviously respectable outlets? To demands for black-and-white answers to overwhelmingly complicated problems?

I think those qualify as 'questions to which the answer is, "Yes"', and we will have a look at them in more detail later. It is fair to say that some of this is art not science: some stories matter greatly, such as Partygate, but not every single time they're mentioned; others, as with Keir Starmer's troubles over Beergate, are initially underplayed and then catch fire. But for now, let us proceed on the basis that news on public service channels should be about informing and enlightening its audiences. There are plenty of other places in the media to entertain them.

CHAPTER 3

REINVIGORATE IMPARTIALITY

Fifty years after my night-time media consumption in Yorkshire, and half a world away, I spent an idle couple of evening hours in Los Angeles flicking between the American news channels – mainly Fox News and MSNBC, on the right and the liberal left respectively. Both were a good viewing experience because the US produces opinionated news well. But what was striking, and depressing, was how little common ground there was between them. The news agendas were completely different; the facts were highly selective; and the views expressed would rapidly have led to a row if they'd been brought together in one forum. If you want to know how divided America is, just watch its television channels and the way they stir their different heartland audiences.

There are signs of it happening in broadcasting here, too. *Channel 4 News* continues to have a flavour of *The Guardian*. In radio, LBC has broken with UK tradition by celebrating the idea that presenters can have opinions, though they combine broadly right (Nick Ferrari on the breakfast programme) with generally left (James O'Brien occupying the mid-morning slot) in one station. This interpretation of impartiality was then stretched further on television by GB News, where the presenters are almost all on one side of the fence, thus edging more towards the Fox News model. Piers Morgan tells us nightly on TalkTV that he is 'uncensored'. Outbreaks of personal opinions and increasingly partisan takes on issues can be found all over the airwaves. It's an echo, inevitably, of social media, where impartiality is simply not a thing.

It is also reflected in newspapers. One media specialist wishes we could turn back the tide: 'Let's go back', he told me,

to the days of opinion on the op-ed pages, and news or proper feature journalism everywhere else. Today, newspaper stories are too often prioritised and written in accordance with an entirely predictable political agenda. If something happens that can't be made to fit their worldview, it usually isn't reported at all. Britain's growing tribalism is exacerbated by newspapers' determination that their readers – left-leaning and right-leaning – should see nothing that doesn't compound their prejudices.

Necessarily in these circumstances, when Tim Davie became

director-general of the BBC in the autumn of 2020 he put broadcasting impartiality at the top of his list. 'We urgently need', he said, 'to champion and recommit to impartiality' – which the corporation now likes to define as 'being unbiased'. It is not only the BBC which seizes on the distinctiveness of being impartial. The UK's Sky News is now owned by the American giant Comcast, and I spoke to the channel's head John Ryley, who sees it as 'very much in the public service mix':

> Impartiality is, I would say, good for business. There is an expectation in Britain that serious broadcast news will be impartial. That's not just about seeking a broad range of opinions, but it's also about an attitude to getting facts correct. I sometimes worry that younger journalists in the industry are not quite so clear about that, but being factual and accurate is the core of impartiality.

My former colleague Richard Sambrook concurred in his own take on impartiality when he spoke to a parliamentary committee at the end of 2021:

> Impartiality becomes better and easier to deal with when you start to break it down into its constituent parts … Accuracy, fairness, an evidence base, a diversity of view, transparency of process and those kind of things. When you break those down, you can start to engage with them

more, start to measure them, start to evaluate performance against them in easier ways.

But he also warned that some aspects of impartiality are harder to grasp: 'It is widely misunderstood in public debate as being about false balance, or about covering up your personal opinions, or being bland "he said, she said" journalism. Impartiality, properly employed, is the reverse of that. It is a set of professional disciplines to elevate your journalism beyond personal bias.'

It might also be helpful to define impartiality by a negative, which is that it's about not taking sides on matters of current controversy where the conclusions of well-informed people may differ. (I stress 'well-informed'; it's not just believing any old tat from the fringes of the internet.) Tim Davie's words were an unmistakable rebuke to some of the corporation's staff who were losing sight of this most important of values. 'If you want to be an opinionated columnist or a partisan campaigner on social media, then that is a valid choice,' Davie told employees. 'But you should not be working at the BBC.'

However, the scale of this task is enormous, because what we have witnessed is a long-standing tendency within the BBC to drift towards an unconscious liberalism – in an agreeable Shirley Williams kind of way – being intensified by the cultural sensitivities of recent years. 'Why do we now have an LGBTQ+ correspondent but not a crime correspondent?' asks one presenter. 'You couldn't shout out a more liberal metropolitan agenda if you tried.' Not all the corporation's lacunae are liberal: it has simultaneously managed to be sometimes rather conservative on matters of economics, as it is on the royal family. Views from the radical left were as likely to be unexplored as those from the right. There is sometimes a tinge of the state, which can make the BBC seem pro-government. But there is a strong view among the new generation of BBC executives that for multiple reasons Davie's priority of defending impartiality has become an obligation, not a choice. It is also seen by some in the industry as an issue that is particularly acute at the BBC. One journalist who has worked at the BBC and Sky and ITV thinks the commercial organisations are different culturally: 'The smaller teams there often feel nimbler and more able to deliver news in a punchier way – with less time for groupthink.'

The roots of all this run deep. One of my happiest times at the BBC was as editor of *The World at One* three decades ago. There was an extraordinary string of historic stories, from the fall of the Berlin Wall and the resignation of Margaret Thatcher to the invasion of Kuwait and the release of Nelson Mandela. The job meant long days in a grimy office filled with cigarette smoke, wondering what the world could throw at us next. But what made it fun was the production team: a set of people who were bursting with creativity during production shifts and then ate and drank together during breaks or after work, with a particular emphasis on drink.

We came, at first glance, from many different backgrounds. There was a Protestant from Northern Ireland, and a Catholic from there too. We had a couple of Scots on the team, including our lead presenter James Naughtie. Yorkshire was represented by me and the editor of *PM*, Kevin Marsh. We had team members from ethnic minorities, which was rare thirty years ago. Also unusual in BBC current affairs production: a couple of people with degrees in science. But our similarities were, in truth, greater than our differences. We were almost all twenty- or thirty-something in age. We almost all lived in London. Almost all of us had been to university. It would be wrong to say we had forgotten our roots, but our working lives were in a capital city and our personal bases were typically in suburbs favoured by the upwardly mobile or the established media chattering classes. We had a range of political views, though most were on the moderate left. It was not unknown to find that nice couple Neil and Glenys Kinnock from Ealing at parties hosted by colleagues. In our social attitudes we were supporters of full and equal rights for women, pro-gay, pro-ethnic diversity and we were knowingly divergent from majority opinion on the debates of the day – this being a time when the government had introduced a law preventing the 'promotion' of homosexuality in schools and when elected Sinn Féin politicians were officially banned from the airwaves. We were, for the most part, typical metropolitan liberals.

But the ambient liberalism didn't automatically transfer to the airwaves. There was still enough of a grip of the values embodied by Douglas Stuart and *The World at One*'s own founder, William Hardcastle. A member of my generation of management observes: 'The BBC's liberalism used always to depend on a degree of genuine curiosity at key editorial levels about ideas and views different to – and challenging of – your own.'

I also never came across cases where colleagues tried to subvert the journalism for any party-political advantage. The *World at One* staff were professional, and we were scrupulously fair in the political balance of the programme. The main parties felt they generally got decent treatment, and the few complaints were as likely to come from the Labour Party – Neil Kinnock famously protested: 'I'm not going to be bloody kebabbed' after a tough question from James Naughtie – as they were from the Tories. We had cordial relationships with Downing Street, which allowed us to have New Year's Day interviews for some years with John Major as Prime Minister.

There were, however, unmistakable indicators of how the BBC culture differed from the outside world. On the *Today* programme in the mid-1990s, we hired a charming young chap called Michael Gove as a reporter. Conservatives were by no means unknown at the BBC, and editors knew that we needed to reflect a range of views – Robin Aitken, now a vigorous critic of the BBC from the right, was also a reporter at the time – but the reaction to Gove was telling, in that colleagues found it a novelty to have a proper Tory on board. His political passions were apparent years before he became an MP, and they were a talking point. He had contacts that we didn't – he was close to the Eurosceptic wing of the Conservatives, and in his spare time he was writing a biography of Michael Portillo – and he could be refreshingly argumentative about some of the leftie rhetoric in editorial meetings. But he was a rare anthropological specimen. Later, Andrew Neil was brandished by the BBC as evidence that they really couldn't be a bunch of wet liberals if they employed him. But it was the fact that he stood out which proves the point.

I know from previous ventures into print that some people don't agree with this characterisation of BBC liberalism. In the *New Statesman* in 2021, the Blair-era Labour speechwriter Philip Collins wrote: 'Former BBC executives such as Roger Mosey have been quick to pile on the clichés about liberal metropolitan bias without giving evidence of it.' So let me bring in some support before I attempt to supply more evidence of why the problem might be increasing.

The wise old hand from *Panorama* Roger Bolton, who has presented Radio 4's *Feedback* programme for many years, defended the BBC in 2010 against charges of historical party-political bias. But he went on:

Of course everyone has views. It is undeniable that most editorial staff were, and probably are, of a liberal inclination when it comes to social issues, and that they cluster around the middle ground of the political spectrum. I would also suggest they are predominantly secular as well. We all have biases, the crucial thing is to be aware of them.

One of my friends who has worked at the BBC for more than two decades and is still there – on the centre-left, I would reckon, and by no means a conservative – says this: 'I think the consensus was highly liberal in all my time and places of BBC work, and the assumption was often that no one wanted to hear the counter view that not everyone sees things this way.'

The presenter Andrew Marr, while he was still with the BBC, had gone further in much-quoted remarks made in 2006. 'The BBC is not impartial or neutral,' he said at a seminar. 'It's a publicly funded, urban organisation with an abnormally large number of young people, ethnic minorities and gay people. It has a liberal bias, not so much a party-political bias. It is better expressed as a cultural liberal bias.'

Former DGs were aware something was awry. In his autobiography, John Birt writes that when he arrived at the corporation in the 1980s, the BBC's journalism 'was still trapped in the old post-war Butskellite, Keynesian consensus. Many BBC people found it hard to think of Mrs

Thatcher as democratically legitimate, perceiving her as an aberration ... The BBC's journalists and programme-makers seemed trapped in their West London prisons.' His successor-but-one Mark Thompson acknowledged in an interview in 2016 that 'journalists as a group tend in their personal politics towards the left'.

Most conclusive, however, is that this view has now been validated by a serving director-general. From the start of his tenure, Tim Davie publicly identified metropolitan and London biases as being challenges for the BBC. He has also in some forums talked about the liberal question, and has conceded that small 'l' liberalism is 'probably' part of this too. Davie is too smart to want to start wading through past controversies, so he pitches this predominantly as an issue for the future of the BBC. He has said he wants to double-down and rebuild trust with audiences on impartiality because it's the best route to preserving public service broadcasting.

As an experienced marketing man, Davie is supported by research. Viewers and listeners believe that the BBC has become less impartial, and the BBC rates lower for impartiality than Sky and Channel 4. Only slightly over a half of the UK population – 55 per cent – believe that the BBC delivers impartial news on television. The regulators at Ofcom, who now have oversight of the BBC, note: 'Each year since 2017 audiences have scored the BBC highly for trust and accuracy in news output. However, our audience research also shows that the perception of impartiality continues to be an area where audiences are less favourable about the BBC.'

Here we need to pause for quick counter-arguments. Critics of the BBC's impartiality are on the left as well as the right, and some viewers see it as pro-government simply because ministers appear on the airwaves more often than opposition speakers. As Ofcom also says, qualitative research shows that views on impartiality are influenced by the wider BBC brand, its funding mechanism and its portrayal in the media. ITV News is less likely to have *The Sun* and the *Daily Mail* metaphorically jumping up and down on its head. Impartiality ratings for the BBC's online offering have recently improved. This feeds into a criticism of Davie from the political left that he is only doing this because he was once a Tory himself and he's meekly following what the government wants. It might also seem to be something of an over-correction for the BBC to have simultaneously Davie as DG, Conservative donor Richard Sharp as chairman and former Theresa May communications chief Sir Robbie Gibb as a non-executive director.

There is nothing new, though, in political appointments, and in the mistily diffuse BBC management structure they struggle to influence the culture of the rest of the organisation. Tory Prime Ministers have appointed Tories to chair the corporation; Labour Prime Ministers have appointed Labourites. Under the Blair government, Gavyn Davies was a Labour-supporting chairman and Greg Dyke as DG had been a donor to Labour. On the EBU board I was regularly goaded about BBC impartiality by the Russian representative, who liked to point out that the BBC chairman at the time, Chris Patten, hadn't exactly been neutral politically. 'And remind me, Roger, what the chairman of your "independent" organisation, who was appointed by your government, used to do? Was he, I remember, also chairman of the Conservative Party?' But Patten and most others ended up going native and becoming stout defenders of the corporation.

I was surprised when it emerged that Davie had been a member of the Conservative Party when he was making his way up the career ladder in advertising in the 1990s. I had worked with him for my last eight years at the BBC, including a particularly close period when he was acting DG and I was acting head of television, and I don't think we ever discussed politics at all. If anything, I'd have had him as 'one of us': a media luvvie, with that small 'l' liberal thing going on. We have to assume that he believes what he's saying while also recognising that a drive to impartiality is helpful in BBC–government relations. As one sage observer puts it: 'A "diversity" campaign might have been the right way to oil the wheels of a licence fee settlement with a Corbyn government; an impartiality fiesta undoubtedly seemed like a good play in the face of Nadine Dorries.' Though the reward for this was scant.

There is a further counter-argument about how much this matters anyway. The BBC is liberal and the Pope is a Catholic and all that. Many of the people who conscientiously defend the BBC do so because they like its values (and so do I) and because they believe the BBC is much better than the alternative (and it usually is). But the journalism is the poorer if there isn't enough diversity of thought, and – as I'll go on to explain – important stories are missed. More than that, it is about consent for a universal licence fee, not just from metropolitan liberals but from everyone in the country. If people do not hear their own voices – or if the opinions they hear are all alien to them – then there is no earthly reason why they would want to pay for a public service broadcaster that excludes their particular section of the public.

The reasons this reached a crisis point can be swiftly told. The liberal tendencies among BBC staff had generally been kept in check by firm editorial control, but somewhere in the 2010s this seemed to slacken. A close observer is critical of the top managers of that period:

Some never understood impartiality and its intrinsic discipline. They had an almost comically metro elite view that the BBC was there to Do Good and be on what they saw as the right side of history. Thus the broad church which has always been intrinsic to the BBC was subtly worn away.

It was also around the time that social media became so dominant, and the BBC was incautious in allowing employees to engage pretty freely – particularly on Twitter. There was a school of thought that it was a splendid thing to interact with the audience, in contrast with some European broadcasters who banned their staff from social media; but in the UK interaction often revealed staff views on the political or social issues of the day. It was especially unfortunate for the BBC that its highest-paid presenter, Gary Lineker, was so active on Twitter. I worked with Gary and very much like and respect him, and as a former England captain he could argue that he is a personality in his own right, irrespective of the BBC. But his ardently Remain views during the referendum campaign were unhelpful to managers who were busy telling his colleagues that they should keep their opinions to themselves. A serving executive told me that the end result was that the BBC's social media policy became 'as lawless as the Wild West'.

This feeds in to a commonly held view among senior managers and some editors, echoing John Ryley at Sky News, that younger generations of journalists do not 'get' the traditional version of impartiality. I know plenty of young journalists; many are extremely talented, and it is completely understandable why they find some versions of impartiality alienating. They have a concern about social justice, which is admirable, and they are used to the free-for-all shouting matches of Twitter, or the partiality of The Canary or GB

News. And they have examples in broadcast journalism, where Piers Morgan, undeniably a talented broadcaster, presented hundreds of editions of a flagship ITV breakfast programme without regulators restraining the expression of his personal views.

This attempted redefinition of impartiality has then been compounded by the rise of BBC employee representative groups, with a focus variously on race (BBC Embrace), gender (Women at the BBC) and sexuality (BBC Pride). Their origins were in seeking rights and diversity within the organisation, which are laudable aims, but they expanded their remit into taking views on editorial matters, which is more problematic. Former foreign correspondent Paul Wood recently quoted a senior BBC figure as saying: 'We're fighting our own culture war within the corporation,' and I have spoken myself to managers exasperated by battles with employees about news agendas and the right of some contributors to appear. In fairness, some programme-makers say they've had little input from the groups, and the biggest impact seems to have been on the management floors. 'This is all about software engineers thinking they'd be better programme editors' was the view of one senior executive.

The management partly have themselves to blame for this. To take LGBT issues as an example, in 2018 the corporation announced a ten-point plan to make the BBC more inclusive. As someone who worked in the corporation for more than thirty years, I would say that the modern BBC has always been gay-friendly – both in the number of gay staff and in the portrayal of LGBT issues on air. It now has 11 per cent of staff identifying as LGBT, which is way above the national population average. The famous kiss between Colin and Barry in *EastEnders* happened in 1987, when the AIDS crisis was stigmatising gay men, and the BBC should be proud of its pioneering role.

Some of the ten points in the plan were internally focused and sensible. But the mission creep was there in plain view: 'There was a general feeling', said the report, 'that News and Current Affairs output often presents balanced debates on LGBT issues which were at odds with the BBC's corporate stance on LGBT inclusion, which seemed to be invisible.'

So 'balance' in journalism was no longer as desirable as supporting the corporate stance on inclusion – which was partly drawn up with the help of the campaigning group Stonewall. The BBC corporate press release issued at the time reinforced that 'while important parts of the BBC's output … present balanced and supportive debates on LGBT issues, more could be done to make the BBC's corporate support for the LGBT community clear'.

There is unpicking to be done here. It is simply not the case that everyone within 'the LGBT community' has the same view on matters of public controversy. For instance, Kathleen Stock, the University of Sussex academic who resigned after a battle with transgender rights campaigners about her views, is a gay woman. I also wonder about the linking of 'balanced' and 'supportive' as if they automatically go together. Would the BBC want to start taking a corporate view on court cases such as the Tavistock Clinic's right to prescribe puberty blockers, which the charity Liberty described as positive for trans rights but where there is dissent?

But you can understand the arguments. On the one hand, if the BBC was to offer maximum support to its LGBT employees, or any minority group, it could make that clear on its airwaves as well as in the way it organises its workforce. On the other hand, it is hard to see why the views of BBC employees – who are unrepresentative of the UK population on multiple measures, such as age (they're younger) or education (they have more) – should trump the opinions of the people who pay their wages.

Still, this may just be me being old-fashioned, because the BBC's then director of radio James Purnell, the former Labour Cabinet minister and sponsor of BBC Pride, added his own thoughts: 'In a recent YouGov survey only 51 per cent of 18–24-year-olds said they identified as completely heterosexual. An organisation that appears to have a heteronormative culture is not one that is going to cut ice with them either as a consumer or an employee.'

He thus disregarded others in the audience, such as anyone with a conservative adherence to a major religion, for whom life partnerships being between men and women are literally a matter of faith. The inevitable then happened: BBC Pride members began to object to people who appeared on air putting views contrary to their own. They joined complaints about an item about LGBT rights on the *Today* programme which was balanced in its arguments but did not feature a trans person in its two guests. *The Guardian* reported in November 2021 that members of BBC staff had written to the DG saying that the corporation would be breaching its guidelines if it hosted a debate about the legitimacy of gender reassignment, and that it must no longer offer a platform to the LGB Alliance, which questions some trans rights.

Criticism had even extended to a member of the audience on *Question Time*, who asked: 'Is it morally right for five-year-old children to learn about LGBT issues in school?' It was the word 'morally' that was seen as provocative, and a BBC presenter was quoted by *The Guardian*: 'We are supposed to set things in context – but that doesn't mean accepting a position that is wrong, or failing to call it out as offensive … We are meant to educate as well as inform.'

It's a view. But it does lead to *Question Time* either banning some questions altogether or having Fiona Bruce scold licence fee-payers for their offensive and wrong opinions. I much prefer the comment of the former BBC reporter Barnie Choudhury, who told a BBC review of impartiality a decade ago: 'If we castigate people for speaking out, no matter how uncomfortable their perception, we end up with frustrated people without a voice.'

There is no doubt that the staff groups created friction

within the BBC, though fitfully rather than universally. More than one employee has described their effects at times as 'toxic', and a close observer is sure that sometimes self-censorship took place: 'Senior editors and newsgatherers have felt intimidated by the groups and their "cancel" power, so they did not ask the more challenging questions of stories involving identity politics. More junior managers simply did not feel they would get backing from the top if they stood up to the groups.'

Another observer, still employed by the BBC, gives an acute analysis of what has been behind all these well-meaning but potentially undermining initiatives:

I think the employee representative groups have grown because they were seen as the 'right thing to do', a kind of outsourcing of engaging with the issues: let them have their group, with a benign senior sponsor who doesn't challenge things too much, and that will make us look inclusive without having to really engage too much or having to challenge some of their more extreme liberal views that don't work in a public service organisation. And through this 'outsourcing', we didn't really know what the groups are for or how their limitations will be policed or managed in the context of editorial guidelines and impartiality.

A presenter, who was the subject of criticism by one of the

staff pressure groups, draws a sad conclusion about what happens if internal censors have undue influence over what appears on the airwaves: 'How does it affect the willingness to interrogate issues, explore unpopular opinions or in fact be rigorously impartial? It's our old enemy, self-censorship. Suppression of all but the obvious.'

Many in the corporation recognised the truth of this. One current senior executive confirmed to me that the LGBT task force's editorial recommendations for News were never, in fact, put into effect. I have not come across a presenter or producer who has been asked to make the BBC's corporate stance on inclusion 'clearer'. The link with Stonewall was formally broken, and the 2021 review of impartiality by Sir Nicholas Serota made it unambiguous that staff groups should not be able to stop the fullest expression of public opinion, even if they don't find what's being said congenial. Serota said plainly that staff networks should emphasise 'the primacy of the BBC's editorial values, including impartiality in shaping all content'. An editor, impeccably liberal, whom I spoke to shortly after publication was relieved: 'Clear guidance, long overdue,' they said. The BBC's director of editorial policy doubled down on this in evidence to the House of Lords early in 2022. David Jordan told their lordships: 'We are very committed to making sure that viewpoints are heard from all different sorts of perspectives, and that we do not subscribe to the "cancel culture" that some groups would put forward.'

But is there a way through this that keeps as many people as possible content? I had an enjoyable chat with Marcus Ryder, a former BBC employee and now a consultant at the Sir Lenny Henry Centre for Media Diversity. He believes that BBC employees 'must be able to express their identity', and that indeed is guaranteed by the Equality Act 2010. He would support their right to attend a Black Lives Matter march or a Pride parade, and we agreed during our discussion that so would I as long as they didn't have an overtly political purpose. I can recognise the wish to attend an event where you affirm who you are. But Ryder correctly says that the read-across to a BBC role involves 'a line that is difficult to find' and some case-by-case judgements. He puts it this way: collectively marking the fact that black lives matter is fine; taking a public stance on whether the police should be defunded is not fine. Again, I agree. A Jew or a Muslim can be proud of who they are and show that in some public settings, but they must still be able to arrange a BBC discussion about the Middle East to the highest standards of fairness. That might only be compromised if their public activities had extended to 'expand the settlements' or 'end the occupation' rallies.

So, my personal take is that I strongly support the idea that people can choose their identity and that a workforce should strive for equality, diversity and inclusion. But it is undesirable to translate that into anything that could be interpreted as a public-facing campaign or as a set of edicts about what can and can't be said on the airwaves. I can see that it may be entering uncomfortable territory if we say to an individual employee: 'You have the right to be who you want to be' and then ask them to produce a programme that questions some of those rights. A trans woman working in BBC Sport might find it awkward to produce an item in which the scope of trans women to take part in the Olympics is challenged. An LGBT member of the religious affairs unit would not have gladness in their heart about booking someone who opposes gay marriage in church. But there isn't a difference in principle between that and a religious conservative hesitating to put on air an identity rights campaigner. These are matters of current controversy in which many millions of people take an alternative view to the BBC's internal values, and it would be a distortion of the debate to exclude one side of it.

An uplifting report comes from a former colleague, now in a commercial newsroom. She sees hope in the younger generation of journalists who are emerging:

> They work at a much faster pace and under greater pressure than we often had to, but they do it (most of the time) while keeping their integrity and impartiality. They expect equality of opportunity – which makes for a better social mix in newsrooms – and often have more emotional intelligence. I have a lot of faith in the cohort who are coming through.

That is encouraging, but I talked to other people who find things much more in the balance. One said Tim Davie had not gone far enough in dealing with the BBC's internal lobby groups: 'He should have thanked them and shut them all down.' We still cannot tell who will emerge strongest in the battle between impartiality and identity. The trap for the BBC is if it heads even further in the direction of the *New York Times* or *The Guardian*. They are great newspapers and liberal institutions but unquestionably narrower these days in their choices of contributors and in the views that can be freely expressed. It is a legitimate model for those organisations, and in a fracturing landscape they can express their views and shape the debate as they see fit. But it is not a safe option for a broadcaster funded by everyone in the country. The *New York Times* would probably have a different attitude if it was compulsorily funded by townsfolk in Missouri or Mississippi as well as Manhattan. As Davie said in his inaugural speech: 'This is about whether people feel we see the world from their point of view. Our research shows that too many perceive us to be shaped by a particular perspective.' And that has already had profound consequences on our national life.

CHAPTER 4

LEARN FROM MISTAKES

'**F**or the first time in my life I thought, "Jesus, I really do operate in a bubble."' The political editor of ITV News, Robert Peston, spoke to the Cambridge student newspaper *Varsity* about his experiences covering the European referendum, with some bleak conclusions:

> The thing I was most depressed about in the aftermath of the Brexit vote is that literally out of everyone I know, nobody that I would regard myself as close to either in family or friendship groups voted for Brexit … It's not part of my self-image because I went to a state school and I do the sort of journalism which is about trying to understand everybody.

It is unlikely that he was alone among London-based journalists. It would also be interesting to know how many could truthfully say the opposite – that nobody they knew in their family or friendship groups voted Remain. It's not a new phenomenon. A couple of decades ago I took a very senior BBC executive to lunch at the House of Commons with a prominent Eurosceptic Conservative. It was before the push for withdrawal from the EU had begun, but the MP floated thoughts about how the UK might disentangle itself from Brussels and strike out on its own. After the main course, he popped to the loo. My colleague was beside himself. 'Roger, he is mad!' he said. 'I mean – where do you even begin to start on how barking this is?' We can now see it is significant that he chose to use the word 'mad' rather than saying, 'I disagree with his policies,' and it is a tiny example of how the Eurosceptics were not taken seriously enough, early enough. It illustrates how life in Broadcasting House or in the ITN headquarters in Gray's Inn Road or in Osterley for Sky is different from living in Hartlepool. The bubble is real.

This fed into the failure among the broadcasters in their 2016 coverage of the biggest political story in recent decades. I wrote in the *New Statesman* towards the end of the EU referendum campaign that it had been 'sour and tawdry' – mainly because of the abject standard of the political debate – but that 'it would be wrong to exempt the broadcasters from some responsibility for that'. Some years on, I believe that is ever clearer.

Again, this is something that goes back over decades rather than merely years. So, let's look at how two strands of our national debate came together in those divisive weeks in the early summer of 2016. The first, most obviously, is Europe itself.

I recommend the book *Reluctant European* by former diplomat Sir Stephen Wall as one of the best accounts of the political story of our country's engagement with the European Economic Community, which became the European Union. Wall is a firm Remainer, but the tale he tells is balanced and nuanced – about the flaws in the EU project and about Britain's persistent disengagement from the defining continental debates. Almost no major UK politician consistently sold the benefits of membership to a sceptical public, and one of the most revealing passages in the book is when Wall outlines the coalition agreement in 2010 between the Conservatives and the supposedly enthusiastic pro-European Liberal Democrats. He notes: 'Of eleven coalition undertakings on the EU, ten were negative and only one was positive.' This reflected Lib Dem campaigning for an in–out referendum if more powers were to be transferred to Brussels, and it showed that even Nick Clegg was prepared to temper his Europeanism in the face of voter antagonism.

As for the broadcasters, they – including me until 2005, when I left BBC News – only truly cared about Europe in so far as it was a British political story. The obsession we all had with political process, which I'll come to in later chapters, overrode personal views on the EU. In the 1980s I had been the producer for a monthly set of reports on Radio 4 about the workings of the European Parliament, which involved an enjoyable trip or two to Strasbourg and some exquisite food, but in all honesty, nobody cared two hoots about that kind of output and there was never a sustained attempt to cover European institutions. The weakness of the Parliament within the system, and the secretive decision-making of the Commission, and even worse the Council of Ministers, didn't help. What made the headlines instead, in the press as well as on television and radio, was any battle between London and the rest – from Mrs Thatcher banging the table and demanding her money back, through John Major's Maastricht travails, to the Cameron renegotiation ahead of the referendum.

Even under the pro-Europe Tony Blair, there was the wounding divide with Germany and France over the Iraq War, along with the psychodrama of the PM's battle with his Chancellor over whether we should join the euro. I can remember vanishingly few attempts to offer a balance sheet of positives and negatives arising from our EU membership, and officials from the EU were usually interviewed about London's grievances rather than their own initiatives. Where was 'The Week in Brussels' or *Panorama* programmes about the continent-wide policy issues?

My friend Catherine Barnard, professor of EU law at Cambridge University, is now a regular commentator on the airwaves and in print about the UK and the EU. But her deployment to explain what was going on only really began from 2016. 'Between 2010 and 2016,' she says, 'it was extremely rare to be invited to comment on EU issues. There was very little interest in what was going on in Brussels or in the politics of the union, and I was seldom asked about the practicalities of leaving the EU or about how Britain's legal relationships worked.' Commentary was instead left mainly to the Westminster political correspondents, who focused on divisions within the coalition and the big parties.

The culture within broadcasting management didn't help at all. A recent BBC executive who managed to keep a wary distance from the management mainstream put it like this: 'Few of the people at my level had an understanding of populism or the tide against globalisation or how deeply anti-London great chunks of the English population are. The unconscious tone from the top made it quite hard to raise pro-Brexit views as something to be taken seriously and explored.'

This weakness was all the more damaging because we had not given enough weight to a major change within the Eurosceptic movement in the UK. For many years on *The World at One* and *Today*, I had tried to get Conservative opponents of the EU to say that the logical consequence of their antipathy to Brussels and its treaties and its centralising itch was that they would quit the union – and none of them, not even hardened veterans such as Bill Cash and John Redwood, would publicly accept that. But there were signs that significant numbers of voters were ahead of them. In 2004, the withdrawal advocates in UKIP came third in the UK's

European elections, beating the Liberal Democrats; in 2009, they came second, beating Labour; and by 2014, they were top of the poll, beating everyone. What was happening was a merger of the aims of the Eurosceptic right of the Tories with the populist insurgents of the Referendum Party and then UKIP and finally the Brexit Party.

Now, my recollection is far from perfect. But I can remember few serious attempts pre-2016 to interview at length advocates of leaving the EU about what it would actually mean, and nor was there ever much of an effort to ask the politicians who advocated a referendum what they would do if the Leave side won. Leave had become an end in itself, and analysis of what post-leaving relationships with the EU and the rest of the world would look like was non-existent. It was easy enough as a political play for David Cameron and Nick Clegg to say they would give people an in–out choice; but by offering that they were accepting, by definition, that leaving was possible. The absence of a plan is as much a charge against the Remain side as it is against Leave. The one conspicuous example of taking the debate seriously was the series of encounters in 2014 between Nigel Farage and Nick Clegg – starting with a broadcast on LBC and followed by one on the BBC – in which all the signs were there.

Farage won by a mile: in the first debate by 57 per cent to 36 per cent, and in the second, according to YouGov, by 68 per cent to 27 per cent. Clegg was afterwards reported by *The Guardian* to believe that 'he could not turn the

Eurosceptic tide in the UK in two hours of debate', though that was presumably his motivation in offering the debates in the first place – and it underlines the failure of Remainers to prosecute their case even when they are, to take a random example, Deputy Prime Minister of Great Britain and Northern Ireland.

One voter afterwards told the news bulletin about her reaction to one of the debates:

> Both sides fire a lot of facts and figures at you, which they bandy around. Facts and figures, in the end you believe what you want. They are both as convincing as each other. That's the problem. And you don't know quite – well, I can't make my mind up – which side is being honest with these figures.

This is revealing precisely because there are indeed facts and figures, and versions of 'their truth' are bandied around gaily by both sides. It is the job of broadcasters to deconstruct them and tell the audience what is what; and the mainstream media failed in 2014 just as they were to fail in 2016. It's important to say here that all broadcasters will be able to show that they did something somewhere during the years of debate about each of the relevant issues. There is always a fact-check or a sceptical note in a piece, or a Radio 4 programme tucked away in the schedule which tried to explain an issue. But the inadequacy was in the coverage of Europe in the headlines and top stories of the biggest bulletins across all channels, where there wasn't enough determination to tackle the partisan agendas of Fleet Street and Westminster.

The other major strand of national debate which had been inadequately covered was immigration. I write as a firm supporter of immigration. I grew up in Bradford, already in the 1960s one of the most diverse cities in England, and I have lived most of my adult life in London, culminating in working on the Olympics with its celebration of a multi-racial Britain. I'm now a resident of Cambridge, which every day shows the benefits of a global reputation through an international body of students and academics. But I also know that if you drive up the road to Peterborough or go to the coastal towns of Norfolk or Lincolnshire, you will find a different view of immigration and one which, for many years, was under-represented on our national airwaves.

There are plenty of reasons for this – some good and some bad. In his *New Statesman* piece in 2021, Philip Collins criticised me on these grounds: 'The BBC should reflect all the opinions of the country, Mosey argues. It would, in fact, be illegal for the BBC to reflect back the racism sincerely held by a fraction of the population. The BBC is not simply a mirror in which the nation sees itself.'

Actually, I do think that the BBC should be a mirror in which the nation sees itself. I am also 100 per cent against fostering racism or allowing illegal hate speech on the airwaves, and I trust the overwhelming majority of the British people not to do that. But I am in favour of there being a rational debate about immigration policy, in which all legal views can be expressed. It is dangerous to start from the position that we'd better not ask people, just to be on the safe side.

This is a discussion we had within the BBC in 2003, when, as head of television news, I and other editors took issue with some views from a corporate editorial policy meeting. The meeting had criticised some of our output, saying that it wasn't 'understanding' enough about asylum and was over-doing 'stereotypical' images of refugee camps in France. The minutes said that this was 'an area that is being led by an angry tabloid agenda and extreme right-wing groups'. That was true; some of the coverage in the newspapers was reprehensible. But this required a dispassionate, fact-based BBC to move it up rather than down the agenda. Asylum and immigration had traction because concern ran widely across the population. It wasn't about what Nick Griffin and his odious British National Party or the other racist extremists of the day felt: it was ordinary people across the UK being worried about the numbers of people coming into the country because of what they believed was the effect on housing and schools and the health service and the rest. 'I think it was also about identity,' notes one academic researcher who spent some time in Brexit-supporting territory. 'It was people saying their town wasn't their own any more.'

There is an excellent long read on *The Guardian*'s website

by Nicholas Watt and Patrick Wintour which shows the scale of this. In 1997, net immigration stood at 48,000 per year. They go on: 'Between 1997 and 2010, net annual immigration quadrupled, and the UK population was boosted by more than 2.2 million immigrants, more than twice the population of Birmingham. In Labour's last term in government, 2005–2010, net migration reached on average 247,000 a year.' Specifically on the effect of allowing free movement and the right to work here for people from the countries which joined the EU in 2004, the *Guardian* authors say: 'Virtually all politicians now agree that the failure to impose transitional controls was a mistake.' They quote the former Labour minister John Denham as calculating that 14,000 Eastern European immigrants had arrived in his home city of Southampton over an eighteen-month period. He is reported to say now that 'on EU migration there was a catastrophic failure of the civil service machine'.

A lot of this was subterranean even in government, so it's not entirely the fault of the broadcasters that they didn't clock what was going on either. But it is rather counter to the aim that the BBC said it had in the 2000s of focusing on grassroots issues around the UK and putting them on the national agenda. I was not alone in thinking that we had missed the public worries about asylum and immigration: my former colleague Helen Boaden spoke of an 'extreme liberal bias' on immigration being apparent before her move to BBC News. The contributions from the regions tended to be translated into subjects we were more comfortable with, such as opposition to fly-tipping or concerns about the environment.

The absolutely essential point here is that this is not about enabling racists or racism. It is precisely the opposite: it is about fostering a rational discussion and making the facts known. The racists can howl away on social media, as they do, but the public broadcasters can provide the best platform for all sides to make their case and to try to identify where the truth rests. As the astute observer Sunder Katwala, director of British Future, wrote in 2014 after the Clegg–Farage debate:

Claims about mistrust, betrayal and even a conspiracy of the elites are a key motivator of one side of the argument. This is also true of immigration, where the public have also heard governments of both colours say that the system is broken and not fit for purpose, and believe this to be true.

So, this was never going to be easy. But what was ignored too often was investigating the complexity of the immigration picture, and also allowing the case to be made *for* immigration. There are considerable benefits for the economy and for our culture, but instead the focus was on that 'broken' system through the usual prism of Westminster politics.

Until 2016. And what happened in those unsettling weeks

of the referendum campaign was that the two under-explored strands of leaving Europe and controlling immigration came together – with predictably terrible effects. I will note here for transparency that I was a Remain voter, and Leave voters may be tempted to dissent. But it is a matter of fact that at least some Leave campaigners gave the impression that we could both leave the EU and stay in the single market, without qualifying what that would mean in practice. And they also played the immigration card throughout, including the introduction of what they saw as the trump card of future Turkish membership. That's even without the notorious bus proclaiming that we sent Brussels £350 million a week, which was simply wrong. By contrast, Remain were on firmer ground with their facts – though they discredited some of their campaigning by the over-egging of their Project Fear.

What was doubly unfortunate was that, perfectly properly for a campaign within a regulated environment, the mainstream broadcasting in the UK went into election mode with a strict division of the airtime 50 per cent between Remain and Leave. But they went further into what I've termed 'robotic balance', in which one side popped up with one view and the other side popped up with the opposite – and the correspondents did not usually counter with the facts of the situation or introduce an expert view. I wrote at the time about a typical piece: 'When JP Morgan announced that it might move 4,000 jobs out of Britain, one peak-time TV package included a clip of the bank; a yah-boo response by Farage; and then interviews with people on Bournemouth beach about whether they thought it might happen.'

Clip of a pro-Remain voice, tick. Clip of a pro-Leave voice, tick. Vox pops to give the thing a bit of life, tick. (Bournemouth beach was chosen because JP Morgan are based locally.) But would anyone have been any the wiser about what investment banks might actually do or what effect EU membership had on our banking system? A cartoon voters' guide, published at the time by 5 Live, was equally even-handed – and unhelpful. On the future of jobs, inside or outside the EU, it advised that 'there's no right answer'. 'Is [leaving] a risk?' asked the presenter, before concluding: 'Maybe there's a risk however way you choose.'

One well-known radio presenter told me, despairingly, at the time: 'Balance has too often been taken to mean broadcasting televised press releases. Instead of standing back and assessing arguments, we have been broadcasting "he says, she says" campaign pieces, which rarely shed any light on anything.'

Four years later, Robert Peston summed it up perfectly, I thought, in his lecture on impartiality:

As someone who worked with immense pride for the BBC for a decade, I watched with disappointment the corporation's coverage of the referendum. Because … it felt to me that the BBC was confusing balance with due impartiality.

Balance, or hearing a range of competing views, is of course important. But the duty of the reporting journalist is to weigh up those competing views and say that on the weight of the evidence this or that view is more likely to be correct. It was no service to the BBC's viewers and listeners to hear one business leader or economist say Brexit would make us poorer, and another say it would make us richer, and then not be given help by presenter or journalist in assessing which was more credible ... Among the many things that I wish in life, I wish the BBC was more confident in its news coverage.

Peston maintains that he did that by consistently saying on ITV that leaving the EU would make the UK poorer: 'Not massively poorer. I thought the Project Fear bit of the government's campaign was overdone. But poorer.' It may be significant that the Vote Leave campaign made a formal complaint about ITV's coverage – which was later dismissed by Ofcom. My editorial guidance, if I'd still been in a newsroom at the time, would be similarly to say on air that if voters were motivated by wanting a stronger economic outlook, then the overwhelming view of economists was that would be better achieved by staying in the EU and the single market. However, if you were motivated by a desire to take more control of UK political decisions – including on immigration – then that would be better delivered by voting to leave.

Most of all, though, it is about giving the facts where they exist. The figure on the bus about our payments to the EU was identified as inaccurate at the time by BBC Reality Check. It had an admirably robust conclusion: 'Leaving the EU would not give the UK an extra £350 million a week to spend on the NHS.' But the bus was still allowed into a multitude of shots with its slogan across our screens, and there was not enough challenge to the politicians. Tom Bradby of ITV News was the most honourable exception in his interview with Boris Johnson aboard the bus as it hurtled through the countryside. Bradby pulled no punches, starting with a graphic explaining the real figures and telling Johnson about the claim of sending £350 million to the EU: 'We don't, and you know we don't.' It was, Bradby said, 'misleading' and 'ludicrous', and the side of the bus essentially represented 'a dirty great lie'. The BBC cited a more polite encounter between a *Newsnight* presenter and Douglas Carswell of UKIP (but significantly nothing featuring Johnson) as evidence that they were on the case. That proves it was not tackled consistently enough.

My former colleague Mark Damazer, who served as deputy director of BBC News, added a stricture in a piece for the *New Statesman* in 2018:

There was, and is, almost no attempt to compare the [£350 million] sum with public spending as a whole or even GDP. So politicians parrot that we are 'taking back control of our money' as part of the elevator pitch for Brexit, when the question is: how much money? The answer, even before the rebate of around £80 million a week is taken into account, is less than 2 per cent of public expenditure and much less than 1 per cent of GDP.

Equally, I can see no reason not to have been clearer that the chance of Turkey actually joining the EU – or having an immediate policy of complete freedom of movement – was vanishingly small. It should also have been possible to land more blows on George Osborne's economic predictions. We now know what happened in reality, and one suggestion is that his worst forecasts were too negative about growth by 5 per cent of GDP. After the referendum, an all-party committee of MPs criticised the politicisation of Treasury reporting, which they said 'misrepresented the analysis and was very obviously partisan in the context of the campaign'.

I tested some of these arguments when I appeared with my former colleagues Richard Sambrook and Sarah Sands before a House of Lords committee in December 2021. In its reporting of the session the *Press Gazette* tweeted that I had said: 'During the Brexit referendum, there was a rather robotic impartiality that wasn't very helpful in terms of guiding people to facts … Impartiality doesn't mean being bloodless.' Predictably, somebody replied immediately: 'Roger Mosey regretting he didn't try to tip the balance in favour of Remain.' So, it is worth underlining that in saying this I am not advocating that the broadcasters should have taken sides; they should have remained absolutely impartial about whether Remain or Leave came out as winners. But given the importance of the decision facing the country, broadcasters should have been more active in inserting the facts and giving measured analysis to the electorate. This should happen on all stories, all the time. It happens, I think, that more of the dodgy campaign stats and untestable claims were made by the Leave side of the argument, while the Remain campaign was plain weak. I asked a prominent Brexiteer what he made of this thought and, no fan of Boris Johnson, he replied: 'What do you expect in terms of a commitment to telling the truth when Johnson is involved?' Other Leave leaders, he believed, behaved more responsibly.

I should also report what one of the enablers of Leave, Dominic Cummings, said in a tweet some years later: 'What I find darkly amusing is how five years later the Remain Establishment still bang on re. 350/Turkey instead of asking, "How did we call a referendum we didn't need to then blow it so badly?"' He added: 'If ppl like DC [David Cameron]/ Heywood [Cabinet Secretary Jeremy Heywood] knew what they were doing, 350/Turkey would never have been enough. Remain could/should have won 60–40. Extreme delusions + incompetence blew Remain up. Then they didn't learn and let us pull a similar heist in 2019.'

In other words, the Leave campaign knew exactly what they were doing – and to want to win is politics at its most raw. It was in plain sight. It's not the broadcasters' role to stop people voting in the way their heads or hearts tell them to, but their duty is to ensure that the public's calculations are based on accurate data. Cummings seems to accept that a level playing field with two equally competent campaigns would have come up with a different result.

The other failure by broadcasting managers was not to challenge the agenda of the respective campaigns. Again in the interests of supposed fairness, the landmark political debates tended to be about the economy, because Remain liked that territory, and immigration, because Leave favoured that subject. That counted as balance, and the Wembley debate two days before the vote majored on these two themes. But it didn't have to. It could have been about Northern Ireland and the border, which went on to dominate our lives for many years after Brexit and which was sitting there unexamined during the campaign. Instead, when Tony Blair and John Major went on a visit to Belfast to raise the issue of the complexity of disengagement, the story was treated as a bit of political knockabout, with balance provided by the DUP's Arlene Foster saying they should have stayed at home. As I wrote in the *New Statesman* at the time: 'As a voter, if you wanted to know what role the EU had played in the Irish peace process, or what the analysis might be of the risks ahead, you were given no clues.'

The net result, as the BBC's political editor at the time Laura Kuenssberg said on 6 June 2016, was that for voters who are only just tuning into the EU referendum debate they might take one look and tune out again. What they might see this morning – one side accusing the other of being a bunch of liars who you wouldn't trust to feed your cat, the other side claiming the others include bitter has-beens and a load of sneering patricians telling you they know best.

She went on to do rather a good piece of analysis about why misleading figures are being used: 'As Leave again publishes a group of numbers that don't quite stack up about future EU bailouts, it's worth bearing that in mind. It's a tried and tested strategy in politics – if you want to make a point – make a row.'

But the point remains: who enables that row? Is it the law that the row must dominate the broadcast media, or could the agenda be chosen differently? In particular, it is seriously odd that the deconstruction of some of the Leave statistics by the BBC's Reality Check – linked to by Kuenssberg in her blog – too often failed to feature in the main bulletins or the landmark interviews. The connections were inadequately made.

Kuenssberg then came, I would say, to the wrong conclusion: 'The question in the months to come is if the referendum rows have got so bad they have destroyed voters' faith (even further) in the politicians involved.' Actually, the question in the months and years to come was whether we had voted to leave – a decision which will define the UK for generations – based on the facts. Much was made of the top UK Google search the day after the referendum being 'What is the EU?' Most of the blame sits with the politicians, but the broadcasters can't understate their role here. They determine the content of what we tune into. They choose how the debate is presented. They can have a policy about what matters and what doesn't and what are the salient facts. And in the EU referendum, they didn't get that right.

CHAPTER 5

KEEP QUESTIONING WHAT YOU DO

There are some stories where conclusions can be firm. On others, it's too early – or we may lack the expertise – to come to definitive judgements. But it is always right to challenge assumptions and test arguments if a huge story is still going on, especially when it's still possible to make some corrections to the narrative. This must be the case with the global pandemic, and as I write this I am keeping an eye on the shocking pictures and courageous frontline reporting from Russia's invasion of Ukraine.

In the early days after Russian tanks rolled into a democratic European country, there was a debate about whether we had 'joined the dots' sufficiently regarding Vladimir Putin and his state. The timeline takes on a more sinister dimension with the virtue of hindsight. A war with Georgia in 2008, followed by ethnic cleansing and grave abuses of human rights. The annexation of Crimea in 2014, with continuing conflict ever since. The locking up of members of

Russia's opposition and the murder of other enemies. The alleged attempts to rig the 2016 United States presidential election, and others. The Salisbury poisonings, which brought biological warfare to the United Kingdom. And despite this, we took part in a Winter Olympics in Sochi and then a FIFA World Cup across Russia in which the host country was portrayed mostly as a confident emerging society recovering from decades of communism. The sports coverage and its presenters barely mentioned human rights.

The analysis must be at its sharpest for Western governments: did they do their duty in seeking to contain the Russian threat? But there is some soul-searching to be done for the broadcasters too, and for all of us as individual electors, about whether we spent enough time worrying about the geopolitical threats to this country and its alliances. It is another under-explored consequence of leaving the EU, and a topic which was barely discussed during the referendum campaign. Equally, Donald Trump's tub-thumping about NATO countries paying 2 per cent of their GDP towards defence was always seen as the President being his usual erratic self, especially given his own Russian connections. Later, even a reluctant Germany acknowledged that the 2 per cent target was right.

Moscow-based correspondents did try to tell the story well, and they were often under considerable pressure. Some were expelled from Russia. But the broadcasters should be asking themselves whether they gave enough time and prominence to making the connections between a massively armed, repressive regime in Moscow and its relationships with the rest of the world. Part of that is within the brief of foreign affairs teams in London and specifically defence correspondents – but at one point the BBC proposed scrapping that role. So, as social affairs issues proliferated in running orders, the voice of the defence correspondent was diminished. One former holder of that role at the BBC, Mark Laity, a fellow producer on the *Today* programme in the 1980s, puts it like this: 'Defence is not a salient issue most of the time, but when it is: nothing is more important. What the BBC has done is misplace its role and seek to be trendy – rather than recognising global trends and reporting on them in an expert way.'

Laity believes most of the cutting-edge defence journalism is now with the newspapers:

> To be blunt, defence reporting has declined overall, but the newspapers wipe the floor with the broadcasters – and at the start in Ukraine the BBC was usually lagging the rest. I was channel-switching furiously and have mostly got more out of Times Radio than BBC Radio, and as a former BBC man I truly hate to say that.

Defence is just not a subject that has fought its way onto the television bulletins in normal times. It would be an interesting research task: how many pieces on the news urged higher spending on the health service and welfare compared to the number of items suggesting we should buy some new tanks? It was left to the Polish politician Radek Sikorski to explain on *Question Time* just how far the West had disarmed in recent years: there were 250 tanks in the German army; 240 in France; 200 in the UK – and 13,000 in Russia. 'We have to stop consuming the peace dividend,' he told the audience. 'Because peace is over.' How much earlier should we have spotted that? Instead, it was a dormant political issue except when it was used as a way of questioning the patriotism of Jeremy Corbyn, who never had any time for NATO.

When the threat to Ukraine was crystallising, the correspondents struggled to get the perspective right. 'Boris Johnson humiliated by brutal Partygate question as he tries to stop Ukraine war' was the headline in one newspaper after the Prime Minister was asked at a pre-war news conference in Kyiv – alongside Volodymyr Zelenskyy – why he had been answering questions in Parliament about Sue Gray's report rather than speaking to President Putin. 'Boris Johnson squirmed on the international stage,' wrote a British journalist, without noting that it was another British journalist who had travelled to Kyiv and chosen to prioritise that question. Time after time during the build-up to the war, the political correspondents' fixation on process swung into sight, with analysis saying that Johnson was using foreign affairs as a distraction from domestic turmoil; it felt that his ill-fated birthday cake was analysed more than the decisions on armaments and logistical support for an em-battled people.

This fits into a pattern in which governments and the media are bad at long-term planning. Programmes respond promptly to breaking news and delve excitedly into the controversies of the day. Ministers favour the quick hit that makes them look good over the quiet decision that makes us safer in ten years' time. So, did they spend enough time planning for a potential energy crisis? Or preparing for the extreme weather events brought about by climate change? And how much airtime was devoted to a national health-care plan designed to tackle the endemic diseases and structural inequalities in Western countries, let alone to debating before 2020 whether pandemics might still be a grave threat?

Yet for all that, the media's treatment of the global corona-virus health emergency is exhibit A in the merits of mature journalism over the chaotic, panic-inducing misinforma-tion of social media, and from the outset I often praised the broadcasters' coverage. I wrote in the *New Statesman* in March 2020, just ahead of the first lockdown, that 'the BBC's editorial coverage of the coronavirus has so far been strong. Amid a blizzard of information, its correspondents are measured and responsible.' A couple of weeks later, I said: 'The BBC's success in recent weeks has come through doing what it should always have done: being the nation's authoritative and sober source of news, and putting public information and education ahead of ratings.' I admired the reporting of the health emergency by ITN and Sky very much too – and this is in contrast to Brexit, where I wrote at the time about the inadequacy of the coverage. We should never forget the context: in Covid we were facing the unknown, and at a time when most of us were confined to our homes, with fear and despondency enveloping our land, it was the reporters and producers and technical teams who kept the public information services going.

The audience demand was obvious. In its annual report for 2020/21, the BBC gave itself a deserved pat on the back:

> Number one source for information on Covid-19: 45 per cent of people named the BBC as their most important source of information/news about the pandemic – far ahead of the next nearest (officials, 13 per cent).
>
> We regularly cleared the schedules to screen vital public information announcements – 84 per cent of adults in the UK came to our services on days when important plans were being laid out.

So, the questions are not designed to undermine those achievements. Rather, they're seeking to identify what we might collectively have missed, and how we can learn the lessons and apply them to the stories that will envelop us in the future. One experienced broadcasting practitioner puts it this way:

Did we challenge ourselves enough? [With Covid-19] we were going into the unknown, and we had never covered anything on this scale before. But if we want in the UK and in other Western countries to be offering the best journalism we possibly can, there are questions, questions, questions that we should be addressing.

The first is pretty basic. Covid-19 was, and still is, a global health emergency – but did the broadcasters make the connections consistently enough? There was one late evening when I watched a UK domestic bulletin in which the main stories were the shortage of PPE, the crisis in the care homes, the fear in local communities that people had been abandoned and a sense that the UK national government was floundering. I then switched to the NBC *Nightly News*, where the main stories were the shortage of PPE, the crisis in care homes, the fear in local communities that people had been abandoned and a sense that the United States federal government was floundering. There was brilliant reporting as the crisis moved around the world, from the early horrors in Italy to the later overwhelming of the health services in India. But were the common themes, the events that were happening everywhere simultaneously, identified strongly enough? For instance, with the exception perhaps of New Zealand and some other countries in the Asian Pacific, was there any democratic government that didn't struggle? There were unquestionably mistakes specific to individual countries – history is likely to judge that the UK should have locked down earlier in March 2020 – but within the European continent it is hard to identify anywhere with policies that were completely 'right' or 'wrong'.

The second big area for questioning is what we meant by 'following the science'. The phrase ran the risk of over-simplification, as if the scientists were all united and on the same side being wise and noble, while the politicians were on the other side being their usual disreputable selves. But scientists differed and their recommendations changed. Initially it was senior medical officials who told us that wearing face coverings wasn't necessary and might even make things worse. A preventative focus which began by being about regular handwashing later moved to an emphasis on better ventilation. Of course. Brilliant research was underway, and we learned more as we went along.

This was sometimes made more confused by the people selected to speak for science. In the UK, SAGE – the Scientific Advisory Group for Emergencies – was a concentration of experts in their field, but members of Independent SAGE, who often took a harder line about the importance of lockdowns, were featured interchangeably. Meanwhile, everyone became an epidemiologist, even if their specialism was in something different – ranging from behavioural scientists to cancer surgeons who developed certainties on Twitter about the transmission of respiratory diseases. It wasn't just Oxford and Cambridge rivalry that made some of my colleagues in

Cambridge raise eyebrows at output from the Oxford Centre for Evidence-Based Medicine which offered a view outside the mainstream – and you can see why programme producers had a heck of a job of working out who was an expert and who wasn't. It would have been better, with hindsight, to have had more concerted attempts to identify a consensus – what are the experts recommended by experts saying? – and more effective labelling of the status of contributors.

My impression at the time, and now looking back, was that breaking news online and on the news channels might too often have been one scientist, irrespective of who they were, saying one thing and another arguing something slightly different – so the premium for getting a headline was about how optimistic or gloomy your forecast was about the infection rates, or whether you wanted tighter regulations or a burst of freedom. Minute by minute, with the lack of patience which is partly a consequence of 24-hour news, we waited for pronouncements from the scientists on the pandemic. We paid less attention to long-term trends and the wider medical community – what was happening to the people who would normally be visiting their GP to check out symptoms? Was the emptiness of A&E departments a worrying sign? – which meant it was hard to take a holistic view of the pressures on the NHS or the trouble that might be building up. For instance, were the consequences of the lockdowns on mental health debated enough?

I am not remotely an expert here, but people who are have

confirmed that there is a difference between the science of locking down, which involves judgements about timing and the likely pattern of human behaviour, and the science of vaccination, where there is definitive medical evidence about what works. The same protesters may have been parading up and down with banners, but being opposed to the severity and duration of a lockdown is not the same as being anti-vax. I talked about this with a couple of doctors, who still believe that governments were right to use lockdowns in the fight against the virus yet accept that there is a debate about timing and severity. However, they believe that if anything the media could have highlighted even more the consequences for those who refused vaccination. 'I went down a ward one day and every single person receiving special care had not been vaccinated,' said one. 'It would have made a really strong report for the nightly news.'

Former head of BBC journalism Mark Byford has his own wider thoughts:

I wonder whether we heard enough from the economics teams, the social affairs units, the home affairs teams? Did they bring sufficient different insights, rooted in specialist journalism? I think the audience could have heard more about the economic and societal consequences and the texture of the arguments about what the pandemic and lockdown and changes in our behaviour were doing to society.

By contrast, he and I both felt that it was the political teams from whom we may have heard slightly too much. I wrote this in the *New Statesman* in March 2020:

> All the Westminster correspondents tend to see the crisis through the prism of how Boris Johnson is handling it, rather than focusing on the audience's interest in advice for themselves and their families. A political reporter is always on the alert for 'gotcha' moments and U-turns, whereas members of the public may well give credit to officials who change their minds when new evidence demands it. The weaknesses demonstrated by coverage of Brexit and the 2019 general election – the preoccupation with process and personalities over policy – are still lurking.

I stand by that. The Westminster prism was, as ever, unhelpful, and it corrupted some of the debate. It's a view supported by the Science Media Centre, which in April 2022 described some of the lessons learned and noted that 'some scientists were put off engaging with political journalists when their comments were used to fuel political rows in the media rather than in helping explain the science'. Conservatives and Labour were often, in truth, in a very similar position, with Labour slightly more hawkish on restrictions. That was also the case between England and Scotland. Nicola Sturgeon positioned herself as more cautious than the wayward administration in London, though many of the policies and outcomes were broadly the same. One well-positioned observer noted to me that the media obsessed about relatively small differences between London and Edinburgh while being much less concerned about the chasms between policy in the UK, Sweden, Singapore and New Zealand. The consequence was that those in the UK who questioned aspects of lockdown, and lacked parliamentary frontbench speakers, were marginalised, and the international comparisons seldom became part of the British conversation.

'Challenge' of authorities needed to be more sophisticated. It wasn't, as one former senior editor puts it, about 'throwing in a grenade that can't be dealt with' – of which this news conference question to the chief medical officer was an explosive example: 'Can you level with us and, based on your graphs, say how many people do you think will actually die?'

It would have been much more helpful to test the underlying strategies rather than seek impossible responses to panic-inducing questions. And why this mattered was shown in an intriguing feature in *The Guardian* in February 2022 about what experts wish they'd known or done with the virtue of hindsight. Here's Professor Allyson Pollock, professor of public health at Newcastle University, who said she regretted not speaking out against school closures:

We knew almost right away, when the blanket lockdown was introduced in March 2020, that children were the least at-risk group, and their education should have been preserved. I wish I'd voiced this more strongly ... On schools, closures should have been no more than a few weeks. I was dismayed at the position adopted by the teaching unions. There was a lot of fear and emotion, but they weren't looking at the evidence or the circumstances that some of these kids were living in, for whom school is a place of safety as well as education ... The second round of school closures was a disaster for children ... It was really difficult to speak out because it was too politicised. The politicisation was totally wrong in my mind.

It's the most enormous shame if she and others felt that. Children, cut off from school, sometimes in appalling domestic circumstances, were too often the unseen victims of the pandemic while the cameras were, understandably, focusing on the tragedies in the Covid wards. The cut and thrust of the daily political arguments – we spent a lot of time discussing whether Gavin Williamson should be in or out as Education Secretary – seem trivial by comparison.

I was struck by a review in *The Times* by Tom Whipple, one of the best science journalists, of a book by Mark Woolhouse, a professor of epidemiology at the University of Edinburgh. Woolhouse was, relatively speaking, a sceptic about lockdowns, and Whipple wrote: 'Of all the counterfactuals this book presents, there is one I desperately wish we had had: a world in which there had been the sort of nuance Woolhouse wants. Instead, supporting lockdown became a test of virtue and opposition to it became the route to YouTube conspiracy-theory madness.'

Those kind of arguments are still running. They could go on for ever, and I hope they will because they illuminate and help us re-examine what we have been through. In these most harrowing of circumstances, public service broadcasting came through pretty well, and it now needs to work out what was the essence of its strengths and where it could be even better. Those lessons should be wide-reaching and about all the biggest stories of our day.

CHAPTER 6

LAUNCH THE BALLOON

It is an article of faith among countless journalists in the nations and regions that London doesn't really understand their patch. 'They don't have a bloody clue' is how one regional BBC veteran puts it. I used to experience it in my time in local radio, when network producers would try to order us to cover for them a local story that they'd spotted in the national papers and would be undeterred by the explanation that either it wasn't true or they had been offered it a week ago and had turned it down. I am equally sure that, as an inhabitant of Broadcasting House for much of my life, I made the same clodhopping mistakes. The simple fact is that we didn't know as much about Carlisle as we did about Chiswick, and it is impossible to have as much empathy for places you've never visited as it is for where you live.

One former manager in the BBC regions puts it this way:

It's always been a paradox to me that while virtually every

BBC journalist will have done time in local radio, they tend to discount it when they've achieved the heights of a national news desk. We've all experienced the visit from the national reporter, hurtling in to do their piece and disappearing. Or the strange desire to interview someone from a local newspaper on a breaking story, rather than the experienced local radio reporter.

These metropolitan tendencies can be particularly damaging at times of national crisis. A study by Stephen Cushion and Llion Carbis from the University of Cardiff identified failings in the coverage of the pandemic and knowledge about which of the UK and national governments were responsible for what:

On 16 April [2020] … the four-nation lockdown was extended, but once again the focus was on it being a singular UK government decision. Of course, journalists and editors were based in London, England and Westminster, meaning their perspective of normalising UK government decisions was perhaps on display during a highly challenging period of time of journalism. But given they are UK network programmes, which have editorial aims of reflecting audiences right across the UK – not exclusively English audiences – the marginalisation of Scotland, Wales and Northern Ireland represents a significant oversight.

Coverage of the devolved nations has improved markedly since I was on the BBC journalism board, and it needed to. But plenty of us had been aware of the limitations of being based in London. I recall a day on Radio 4 news programmes when heavy snow had blanketed the Midlands: schools were closed, cars were stranded, hospital services were stretched thin. Yet in the capital it was a pleasantly mild and sunny day, and it is hard to think yourselves into the snowy shoes of a paramedic in Birmingham when there isn't so much as a blob of sleet to be seen outside your window. The reverse of this is the point often made by colleagues in Scotland: a few snowflakes on the ground in London used to prompt 'snowline emergency' coverage across the UK networks, they would claim, when they had been routinely dealing with much deeper drifts across the Lowlands, let alone the Highlands, for weeks.

Spool forward from those days to the most recent general election and another aspect of the London-based media was revealed. At 10 p.m. on 12 December 2019, the studio audience assembled in London for Channel 4's *Alternative Election Night* programme emitted a despairing gasp when the exit poll results – showing a Conservative landslide – were revealed, and they booed when the presenters confirmed the news. The channel later claimed that the audience had been chosen with political balance very much in mind, but it seems unlikely that an equivalent gathering in a Tory heartland area – or in the Red Wall that was tumbling to the Conservatives – would have had the same reaction. We might have expected a cheer or two, at least, from Brexiteers.

These are anecdotes, and there could be thousands more, about metropolitan and specifically London bias. It is usually inadvertent but sometimes deliberate – London is our capital and by far our biggest city, after all – and often infuriating to the majority of the population living elsewhere in the UK. What we have seen in recent years, though, is an alarming disconnection between the London-based media and the people they are supposed to serve.

One senior journalist at ITV speaks for many in television and radio: 'Pretty much all of us in the mainstream media misread the Brexit vote and the 2019 general election.' What that meant during the referendum campaign was that the possibility of a Leave vote was not taken seriously enough. And in the same way that proponents of quitting the EU never had their case examined or deconstructed in the years running up to 2016, reports from the campaign trail seldom identified the surge in the public mood that led to a 52 per cent rejection of the European Union on 23 June.

In fairness, some of the Leave advocates didn't see it coming either. Nigel Farage was widely reported to believe they had lost at the time the polls closed, and the news conference with Conservative Brexiteers the following day had an air of shock about it. It was a rare correspondent who got to what was happening below the surface in those weeks of early summer. John Pienaar, then at the BBC, was one, writing on 7 June:

> [Labour] MP after MP has returned to Westminster with depressing tales from their home turf; of door-knocking in staunchly Labour areas where apathy towards the EU question has given way to rank hostility ... Among Labour MPs representing areas which will be crucial to the outcome of the referendum, the nagging fear is starting to take hold that it may already be too late.

There was a feeling, too, that Radio 4's *Today* programme did better than most in getting around the country and distilling the mood. It was there to be found, if you looked in the right places. But I came across a number of former broadcasting colleagues who found their own anecdotal experiences of Brexiteers more enlightening than what they heard or saw on the airwaves. One confidently predicted a Leave vote based on a long conversation with the staff in her butcher's shop. A little more scientifically, former director of radio Helen Boaden, who was a rare BBC creature in spending a fair amount of her time living outside London, believes that some figures working for BBC regions were feeding in this kind of advice. She found a striking contrast between her encounters in Yorkshire and the corporate forums in London, where senior BBC executives thought Remain would win by a mile. When I talked to John Ryley, head of Sky News, he told me that, as a resident of Oxfordshire, he had also picked up the strength of Leave sentiment:

> It's a simple fact that most of our newsrooms across the industry are full of people who live in London, and increasingly many didn't grow up outside London or have family outside London. I remember writing a note probably ten or twelve days before the referendum saying that I thought the vote might be much tighter than the London-based media were expecting, and I got quite a pushback. Very few people believed me.

To illustrate how deeply odd this lack of belief was, we need to travel to the Lincolnshire coast and the small town of Boston. I got to know Boston when I was a reporter at BBC Radio Lincolnshire in the early 1980s. It was a perfectly nice town, where even by the standards of local radio not much happened – and it was almost never on the national map. As part of our job applications for Radio Lincolnshire, we had indeed been asked to consider writing a short essay on 'Lincolnshire – the forgotten county'. Once appointed, the radio station team discovered that it was almost impossible to get a hot meal in the town after 6 p.m., this being a time when you were lucky if you found a solitary Chinese takeaway. Later, a local reporter commented on the way the town had changed:

In the '80s it was very much a Lincolnshire town. Then, on a visit a couple of decades later, I was aware of East European shops, East European languages in the market square. I knew someone who was much in demand to translate from Russian for police and courts, and we were doing stories about teachers needed who could speak Polish.

In 2011, the town briefly hit the headlines when five Lithuanian men were killed in an explosion at an illegal vodka factory. And then, in 2016, Boston became famous as the town that voted most enthusiastically for Brexit, and if you do a quick search on Google, you'll find that it achieved worldwide renown. There are reports from CNBC and the American public radio network NPR, from the *Irish Times* and France 24, and from almost every major UK media outlet. CNBC's report, from 2019, gives a flavour of them all:

> St Botolph's Church, known in typically blunt local parlance as the 'Boston Stump', formerly served as a landmark to sailors arriving at the town's docks. In its neighbouring Stump & Candle pub, cries of 'sh*t', 'fed up' and 'p****d off' ring out when the current state of British politics is mentioned.

There was an anthropological fascination with the people of the town. 'A muscular man with a shaved head and glasses leaned forward emphatically to make his point,' wrote one correspondent, in an epithet that would unlikely be attached to a resident of Richmond upon Thames.

What these despatches have in common is that they're overwhelmingly post-2016. What the reporters did was travel to Boston to find out why opinion had shifted so dramatically from the 1975 referendum, when Lincolnshire voted enthusiastically yes, to 2016, when it rejected the EU by a 3:1 ratio. The *Financial Times*, visiting a few months after the vote, was among those thinking it was obvious: 'The motivation for the Boston vote is not a mystery. Immigration here spiked by 460 per cent between 2004 and 2014, mostly through Eastern Europeans coming to work in low-paid jobs in the fields or processing factories.'

Even though that timeframe ends two years before the referendum, it is hard to find much of substance about what the people of Boston thought ahead of the vote. And yet it was all there: unmissable, really. Charlie Partridge, editor of BBC Radio Lincolnshire during this period, notes that Nigel Farage's UKIP had made strong progress in council elections in the 2010s, winning a number of Boston seats on the county council and then running the Conservatives close in the 2015 general election in the Boston & Skegness constituency.

'UKIP were very effective at putting the blame for everything on the EU,' Partridge told me.

I remember a UKIP councillor assuring our listeners that there would be far fewer potholes in the roads if the UK left the EU … For us as a news team, UKIP and Leave were part of our daily political assessment. The local Tories had pivoted almost entirely to Leave. As the referendum approached, our phone-ins and discussions were dominated by pro-Leave callers. It was difficult to get balance on discussions. I acted as warm-up man for a number of live referendum debates across the county, and the passion was all with the Leavers. Remainers were shocked by their vehemence.

The point makes itself. This was Lincolnshire. Other English counties were similar. But London was different, and the main news organisations were all based in London. They failed to grasp the intensity of grassroots anger and the besetting disillusionment with Westminster – with consequences that became apparent through the referendum. What would have been comic if it hadn't been so tragic was the rush of the media to be wise after the event. I was a judge for the Royal Television Society Journalism Awards in early 2017, and watching the entries about Brexit and its aftermath I was of the firm view that none of them deserved recognition. It was reassuring that my fellow judges agreed with me that much of it had been tone-deaf. The immediate aftermath of the referendum vote sent crews scurrying across Britain to understand what had happened, and there were moody shots of weed-ridden streets in Burnley and the newly mandatory outside broadcasts from Boston. Leave voters were frequently portrayed as furious people in seaside chip shops, demanding that immigrants be sent home. Market stalls were another favourite venue for finding the Leavers. And yet... the 'respectable' towns of England had also voted to leave. Sevenoaks in Kent, as much of a genteel place as you can find, had a higher than average 54 per cent rejecting the EU, and the chip-shop customers of Clacton had comrades in Waitrose branches across the Home Counties. The London fog of incomprehension continued.

But some of the reporting was illuminating. There was a day on the BBC News channel – on 29 June, a few days after the result – when Ben Brown presented live from a rain-sodden Boston. He referred to 'strong views on immigration' as a result of up to 10 per cent of the local population now being from 'new' EU countries such as Poland and Romania. A local Leaver duly popped up to say: 'Bollocks. I don't want them. Send them back home.' There was a section on 'acute pressure on local services, including the hospital'. It was responsible, open journalism; though even then, presumably because it was too late, it didn't look enough at what the compensatory benefits of EU membership might have been. How many of the staff in the Pilgrim Hospital were from the EU? What did the Common Agricultural Policy mean for counties like Lincolnshire? How much did regions receive in EU payments? Were students from local schools beneficiaries of the Erasmus scheme? The full picture only emerged slowly afterwards, and you might wonder: why couldn't we have seen the balance sheet sooner? Setting out the pros and cons fairly and in detail would have been a mile better than letting the cons burrow away underground and unchallenged.

Having had this sobering experience in 2016, it might have been expected that the London-based media would sharpen up their act. But they didn't, much. The 2019 general election was another, albeit less egregious, example of a misreading of the country, and a senior radio presenter acknowledges a 'failure to reflect non-metropolitan opinion'. The campaign was often portrayed as close, even though the polls told a story of a consistent Conservative lead. This may have been because it was in the interests of the major parties to claim it was a horserace: the Tories to get their vote out; Labour to maintain morale. Political correspondents love the drama of an unpredictable outcome, too. The result was, in fact, historic: the Tories' best performance since 1987 and Labour's worst result since 1935.

The story of the year was the way the Conservatives moved from an astonishingly low 9 per cent of the vote in the European elections in the spring to a majority of eighty by December, and it was the change of leadership from Theresa

May to Boris Johnson that enabled such a transformation. Love Johnson or hate him, from 2001 until 2019 – his greatest triumph – he won every election in which he stood. Yet Johnson and his Labour counterpart Jeremy Corbyn were often portrayed as equally unpopular. It is true for both of them that their poll ratings as individuals were on the low side, but this led to an underestimating of Johnson's political message: 'Get Brexit Done'. What enabled him to win such a large majority was a combination of his personality – voters thought he'd be an amusing if untrustworthy companion down the pub – with a slogan that appealed so strongly in Brexit-voting areas.

As usual, there were moments when the real story flickered into view. The BBC's Clive Myrie contributed a report early in the campaign from Bishop Auckland, one of the Red Wall seats which was to turn Blue, in which regional political editor Richard Moss unambiguously nailed two problems for the Labour Party: 'Brexit and Jeremy Corbyn.' He observed that Labour canvassers were finding it very difficult to persuade voters to give Corbyn a chance. The *Today* programme's Nick Robinson discovered in his tours that Corbyn's alleged past support for the IRA was a barrier for many voters. Just before polling day, political editor Laura Kuenssberg caused something of a storm for what some saw as a breach of electoral law by revealing indications of postal voting, but she was spot-on in her ad-libbed comments on a live programme: 'The parties – they're not meant to look at it, but they do kind of get a hint – and on both sides people are telling me that the postal votes that are in are looking pretty grim for Labour in a lot of parts of the country.'

It would seem probable, though, that media organisations centred in Durham or Dudley would have been better placed to breathe the air of the new political climate: they would have been able to get the analysis right more often. You can see exactly the same phenomenon in America. The news media are based in New York; the entertainment industry is based in Los Angeles. Which were two of the states that Hillary Clinton won by a landslide in her 2016 contest with Donald Trump? They were, inevitably, New York and California, and there would have been a firmer grip on what was happening in America if more of its media executives knew about Wisconsin.

I titled this chapter 'Launch the Balloon', so I'd better explain it. We did sometimes discuss in the newsroom how we could reflect the UK fully in all its diversity and complexity. Many of us still remembered the BBC One logos in which a hot air balloon drifted over the landmarks of our nations and regions. So, the idea took hold that it was an example of how we should attempt to view the country – not seeing ourselves as confined to a newsroom in London but taking a perspective on everything that was going on in cities, towns and villages and selecting the most interesting stories irrespective of geography. It's not that simple, of course, and we demonstrably didn't achieve it. But it is something to aspire to – a determination not to be metropolitan, not to be captivated only by what's happening somewhere we know.

Otherwise, the alienation of consumers of media from outside London will only intensify. And that brings us back to the weather and the experience at the end of 2021 of thousands of people in the north-east of England, who were left without power for days because of Storm Arwen. There was network news coverage, of course, but without the prolonged prominence or impact it should have had. In *The Spectator* James Kirkup spoke for family members literally still in the dark in Northumberland:

> It's a small place, far away, about which we know little. But the fact that the situation ... is almost unknown to people beyond the north-east still strikes me as notable, and telling. One thing it confirms is that the UK media as a whole has retreated, badly, from regional and local coverage. When journalists generate 'content' by sitting at a desk and staring at Twitter all day, it's too easy to miss significant events in the boring old non-online world. Especially the rural bits of it ... Is it remotely conceivable that such a situation could have gone almost entirely unnoticed in the imperial capital, London?

From power cuts in Northumberland and snow in Birmingham through to Brexit in Boston, the pattern is established. The problem is known. Some of the remedies are already in place, but there's an ever more demonstrable need to burst the metropolitan bubble.

CHAPTER 7

VANQUISH VOX POPS

It might seem that one of the best ways of getting a sense of the UK is to put its people on air – and that is what happens every night on the news. But it does depend how it's done. There is routinely one story, and perhaps more, in which a reporter goes out onto the streets and asks Joe and Joanna Public what they think. These contributions are known as vox pops, and the *Observer* columnist Catherine Bennett gives an idea of their journalistic rationale: 'Annoying hole in your programme or article? Vox pop. Too London-y? Vox pop. Low on colour, no time to wrangle with combative contributors? Vox pop.'

At their least annoying, vox pops can be a break from the politicians and experts who dominate the rest of a bulletin. But most of the time they are a spurious attempt to gauge public opinion and add little to the sum of human knowledge.

Some of this is for a decent reason. They are an example of a particular view of impartiality in action. On controversial matters, journalists are encouraged to reflect both sides of the story – and therefore a traditional vox pop will feature someone saying that criminals should be sent to prison for longer; another arguing that current sentencing policy is too tough; and another saying something non-committal or vaguely amusing. Balance is taken seriously, and I remember one occasion when a reporter had his first version of a piece rejected and was sent back on a 100-mile round trip because he had not found a suitable pro-Tory voice in a Labour constituency in the north-east of England.

But this points to what's wrong. It may be that the overwhelming balance of opinion in that constituency was to stick with Labour, just as on the prisons argument it could be the case that most members of the public favour harsher sentences. You wouldn't know that from the 'A says white, B says black, C says grey' structure of most reports. But there is the opposite problem if vox pops are all on one side: how would anyone know, without proper empirical polling, that the dozen people approached by a reporter on a wet Wednesday are in any way typical of their locality?

Mark Damazer, a former deputy director of BBC News, developed the argument about representing the electorate, based on the Brexit debate then still rumbling, in a 2019 article for *Prospect*:

Mostly on television news, it is done terribly. A recent example from Mansfield told me nothing of any use about the town – unemployment, housing, school quality, waiting times for NHS appointments, culture – but inevitably ended up with two ex-miners (reach for the cliché) in a working men's club (reach for another cliché). Yes, they surely should be heard. Indeed, I would rather hear them at greater length – but there is no polite challenge or commentary in these pieces about the statements made. The reporter, who normally can be expected to know little or nothing about the place, has harvested their balanced soundbites, has dutifully proved that 'real people' are fed up with it all, fled, and filed their report.

His point about Mansfield being a cliché is that it remained a London newsroom trope that it was really only poorer voters who had opted for Brexit. As Damazer added: 'Such pieces don't come from the prosperous south – where outside the M25 Brexit votes piled up in 2016 … The automatic choice is to go "poor".'

It's an important observation about challenge, too. During the pandemic, members of the public were frequently asked about their views on the lockdowns and how they thought the government and the NHS were coping with things. But they were very seldom challenged about their own behaviour. We know that one of the drivers of infection was some people breaking the rules, but lockdowns were usually portrayed as something inflicted on an innocent citizenry by Whitehall rather than a consequence, sometimes at least, of our own actions.

On other occasions, members of the public are asked questions to which the honest answer is 'I don't know' and where the editorial decision to seek vox pops looks eccentric. After both Keir Starmer's and Boris Johnson's leaders' speeches at their 2021 party conferences, a hapless reporter was sent out to seek the immediate reaction from voters. Now, the population of the UK is around 67 million, and 32 million votes were cast in the 2019 general election. But the number of people watching the estimable *Politics Live* programme for a leader's speech is low: in the case of Starmer in 2021, it averaged just 270,000. So, the voters who were able to give a detailed reaction were unusual, and I am taking a wild guess that their decision to watch the speech on a conveniently located big screen showing the BBC News channel or Sky News was influenced by a camera crew being with them at the time. It is a largely meaningless exercise, especially because we know the real shaper of views is how the speeches are later edited into soundbites for the bulletins or for social media. Opinion takes time to settle.

I once grumbled about vox pops on Twitter and was challenged by an experienced TV producer, who tweeted back: 'My experience is the great British public are very vocal and think deeply about matters of life and death, liberty and economic necessity.' I agree. But I am sure that those themes are not best encapsulated in ten-second soundbites on a network bulletin.

Radio stations with a high interactive element – local radio, 5 Live, LBC – can give listeners a platform on which they can construct those arguments. And if they are done properly, vox pops on the major bulletins can work, too. There was a superb piece by the BBC's Ed Thomas after the Euro 2020 football final in which he visited Oldham and spent some time on a street where neighbours had been watching the match together. The St George's flags sagged on a rainy day. There was disappointment at their team's defeat but also the authentic voice of decent English people: their pride in the footballers, their opposition to racist abuse, the fun of the journey they'd all been on – and a little bit of gentle boasting. 'Not everybody got in the final, did they? We did.' It allowed interviewees to speak at greater length than usual and about something they cared about. They were the reason for the piece, not a gratuitous addition.

I also admired a film by Lewis Goodall on *Newsnight* during the height of Boris Johnson's Partygate travails. Voters in Bury took part in a focus group, which meant they were allowed to speak at length in a structured way, and their opinions were much more nuanced than the consistently 'furious public' storyline featured elsewhere. Some of them were sticking to the Conservatives and even to Johnson, which some users of Twitter found incomprehensible.

One tweet said: 'I wondered how Brexit vote could be won and Johnson could win such a majority ... Now I know ... No hope for the country.'

Whether you share that conclusion or not, isn't it interesting that to many social media users that wasn't known before? And it's because the voices in Oldham and Bury are too seldom heard at length.

Meanwhile, my amiable Twitter argument with the news producer about the principle of shorter and routine vox pops had concluded with what he thought was the clinching argument. He wrote: 'I give you – "Not another one,"' referring to the celebrated vox pop with Brenda from Bristol, despairing of the announcement of a general election in 2017: 'You're joking! Not another one. Oh, for god's sake, honestly – I can't stand this…' It is true that this was TV gold, with online viewing running into the many millions. However, it cannot of itself justify the thousands of less memorable clips which clutter the bulletins. Brenda has her place, and Ed Thomas's piece certainly does. But that's enough.

CHAPTER 8

REBUILD THE REGIONS

What the nations and regions of the United Kingdom really need to make their voices heard on the airwaves and on the biggest digital platforms is investment – and power. Broadcasting is the best route to keeping local content strong because the regional press is a mere shadow of its former self. My parents were newsagents, and the rhythm of my early life included the vans delivering multiple editions of the Bradford *Telegraph & Argus* through the afternoon and into the evening. Now, many titles have disappeared altogether, while others are produced in journalism centres many miles away from their patch.

At its start, broadcasting was local because that was all that transmitters could achieve. Radio and television began as services for London and were later networked across the UK. BBC Television reached the north of England in October 1951 with the opening of a transmitter at Holme Moss in the Pennines. The first programme, broadcast from London to welcome the new viewers, was called *Hullo Up There*, which suggests a metropolitan mindset is nothing new.

ITV followed, but with a different structure in which various companies were awarded franchises with regional bases – so Granada Television covered the north of England and the east was served by Anglia Television with its shiny knight logo. The marvel about this set-up was that authority and commissioning were devolved. In the heyday of the ITV system, there were five big companies: Granada in Manchester, Yorkshire in Leeds, ATV/Central in Birmingham and a split in London between Thames and LWT. There was local pride, too, in the smaller outfits: Westward in Plymouth and the minnow Border Television in Carlisle. I remember the day when Yorkshire Television opened, heralded by what became its familiar chords from 'On Ilkla Moor Baht 'at', and it felt to a Bradfordian that there was finally a TV service that spoke to me – with punchy local news, entertainment from just down the road and sports programmes which focused on Leeds United and Bradford City rather than Manchester United and Fulham.

I spoke to Ian McBride, who had long experience at Granada, including as deputy editor of its flagship current affairs programme *World in Action*, before becoming ITV network's managing editor. He underlined how editorial decisions in the time of the 'big five' were taken entirely within the programme companies. There was no question of Granada referring a knotty dilemma to someone in London to resolve. The company was, he says, 'highly commercial but also spectacularly good at creating a huge and impregnable wall around its journalism, with an innate sense of what was right'. This extended to defending its own patch. 'The BBC has a motto: "Nation shall speak peace unto nation,"' notes McBride. 'For Granada, it was very much the case that we thought we represented our nation speaking unto London – there was a kind of unilateral declaration of independence for our region.'

The BBC also did regional coverage, of course. When I was first aware of it, our local programme came from Manchester – acceptable, but very much on the wrong side of the Pennines – with the BBC swiftly setting up a Leeds-based alternative when Yorkshire Television started breathing down their necks. But the BBC came across as much more of a network operation from London. Since then there has been many a twist along the road, but essentially ITV consolidated and became one national company – though one senior ITV journalist says the company is still aware of its legacy: 'ITV News is shaped by its heartland ITV audience, traditionally in places like Granada and Tyne Tees, and strong editorial connections with those regional hubs help inform the coverage.'

But the hubs are not what they were and the glory days of big ITV regions – try reading my mentor Austin Mitchell's rip-roaring account *Calendar Boy*, of the early days of YTV's regional news programme – will not be seen again.

By contrast, in recent decades the BBC has invested more in the nations and regions, including prestige projects such as the new buildings at Pacific Quay in Glasgow, Salford Quays in Greater Manchester and Central Square in Cardiff. Despite that, profile is hard to achieve for the regions. Every night the BBC and ITV get excellent live audiences for their programmes, and Aziz Rashid, a fellow Bradfordian and former head of local and regional programmes for BBC North, told me he thinks it's a daily miracle that eighteen national and regional opt-outs happen so smoothly. The headlines and the 'coming up' sequences are customised for each region, and then there is a top-quality programme with cumulative audiences reaching into the many millions. It's part of the fabric of BBC One (as of ITV) from early in the morning to 10.30 p.m. But, Rashid wonders, 'is it so well-integrated that it's taken for granted?'

This has long been regular business, but more recently there have been a series of interventions to shift the balance of the BBC away from London. Channel 4 has followed suit by opening a major centre in Leeds. I have to make a confession, though. When the BBC first got the itch to send its London-based staff to new locations around the country, almost twenty years ago and well before 'levelling up' was a common phrase, as a senior executive I thought the idea was a grisly one. That's not because I don't like the north of England, which would be a weird attitude for a Yorkshire-man. But as director of sport from 2005, I was being asked to put my deeply reluctant staff and their families onto buses making a one-way trip to the Greater Manchester docklands – leaving behind the power centres of the BBC, not to mention Wimbledon and Twickenham and Wembley (all rather key for sport), with the move scheduled to take place a year before the London 2012 Olympics. I wrote grumpy emails to the director-general Mark Thompson, contrasting his plans for Salford in 2011 with our plans for London 2012. I remember one executive trip to inspect the new site in which the mood was sulphurous. We sat in the docklands on a miserable day, with suitably dark clouds rolling in and political games underway among executives about who would really move and who would pull off a great escape. The only moment of any joy was when we jumped on the train back to London and discovered that the buffet car had plenty of chilled white wine.

I was wrong and we were wrong. MediaCityUK has turned out to be a splendid project, housing not just the BBC but ITV and the set for *Coronation Street*. People generally love working there. There are wine bars, just like in Fitzrovia. But what it hasn't done is deliver one of the great aims of the original scheme: to transform the metropolitan mindset of the BBC and to concentrate decision-making outside the capital. Instead, what has simultaneously been created in London is the most powerful building in BBC history. Formerly, the news and current affairs operations were dispersed across the capital: World Service in Bush House, television news in Television Centre, radio in Broadcasting House, current affairs for many years in Lime Grove. It was inefficient, but it did preserve diversity of thought. Many are the senior managers from the corporate centre who ventured into Lime Grove only to be chewed up and spat out, while Bush House was determinedly in a world of its own.

That changed with the rebuilding of Broadcasting House and the move of all the news services – along with network television and radio controllers – into one building with its celebrated postcode of W1A. It may sound like a trivial point, given they had all previously been in London anyway, but the different cultures were weakened and that was an avowed aim: more efficient multi-platform working across services to replace the squabbling tribal leaders of the past. It became much harder to fight groupthink, and it also had a deleterious effect on the nations and regions. It was ever more possible for a London editor to bump into a controller in Broadcasting House and have one of those informal work chats that simply wasn't possible with people in Glasgow or Bristol.

The BBC compounded this with muddled strategies. Originally the idea of BBC Sport and BBC Children's going to Salford was that they were strong self-commissioning departments. They had a solid production base and direct access to the airwaves. That was chipped away in a multitude of ways: first by the pressure to put more work out to independents, cutting the number of in-house producers, and then by tinkering with the management structure. At first, the director of BBC Sport reported to the director of BBC North in Salford, but later their manager became the director of BBC Content, based inevitably in London. There were examples at every level. A producer on a high-volume Radio 4 programme in theory had the right to do a Salford-based edition once a week – but it was overseen by an editor in London who took the final decisions. Even some Salford-based executives limited their commitment to their new base. Second homes in the north and real homes in the south were not uncommon.

Other BBC regional centres fared even worse. *Private Eye* accurately chronicled the moves in and out of Birmingham over two decades, with the Pebble Mill Studios being closed in favour of the Mailbox in the centre of town, which is now in turn being shut down. Programmes have moved in and out with no discernible rationale, and at one meeting in 2012 I was part of the management team being castigated by the BBC Trust for empty desks in Birmingham, when they themselves had recently approved the shipping out of factual programming staff to Bristol. I once had a call from the director-general urging BBC Sport to locate *Sports Personality of the Year* in Birmingham forthwith, because the chairman had spotted that the city was becoming denuded of broadcast content. A case of 'Get Lewis Hamilton to Brum and hope nobody spots there's nothing else there.'

To his credit, Tim Davie has tried to be more systematic.

'Entire departments and news divisions will be moved to Birmingham, Cardiff, Leeds, Glasgow and Salford,' said a breathless piece on the BBC's website in 2021, claiming it was 'the biggest transformation in decades'. Radio 3 would be 'rooted' in Salford. The whole of Radio 1's *Newsbeat* team would be despatched to Birmingham. (Most declined to move.) There would be a new soap opera based in the north of England – presumably pencilled in to the schedule as 'Coronation Farm' or 'Emmerdale Street' – and the proposals overall were claimed to mean that the BBC cumulatively would spend at least an extra £700 million outside London by 2027/28.

Looking at the detail, though, doubts crept in. For a start, not a single member of the executive board would be moving, and nor would anyone from the BBC News board. As for the teams being relocated, it was another example of 'last child to be picked for a sports team' syndrome. The programmes with the least political clout are the ones that end up being sent out of London. Therefore, it is *Newsbeat* heading to the Midlands, not *Newsnight*. I was on the BBC journalism board when we were given an order to send a significant number of people to Salford; we quailed at the thought of telling Jeremy Paxman and his Westminster-savvy team that they should move – and alighted upon the more amenable *Breakfast* television crew instead.

It doesn't go far enough to proclaim, as the BBC did, that the *Today* programme and *Newsnight* will be presented on location more often. This is journalism via an overnight stay in a Travelodge, not a deep-rooted commitment to a region in which employees live and work and educate the kids. The Channel 4 presenters shipped to Leeds still seem bemused by their surroundings. There was a feeling at the BBC of randomness and 'twiddling round the edges', as the broadcaster Jane Garvey put it in *The Media Podcast*. In news, we were told, the climate and science team was moving to Cardiff, while the technology team would shift to Glasgow and the learning and identity team would go to Leeds. But they would answer, still, to the heads of news content and news output in London, who were given more power in the latest restructure. I can testify that many of the staff involved felt unwanted and bruised by these forced moves.

So, the BBC scorecard has pluses and minuses. Yes, there is a demonstrable commitment to the nations and regions. Yes, real money is being spent. Yes, the daily regional news programmes are successful and valued. Aziz Rashid pointed out to me the happy outcome that breakfast television had come to 'somewhere it was loved' in Salford, when it had previously been marginalised in Television Centre. And network bulletins are hugely better than in my day at capturing the differences in the devolved nations, with notably good contributions by the likes of Sarah Smith when she was Scotland editor. But London still makes all the big calls.

I asked former BBC Lincolnshire editor Charlie Partridge for his perspective. On the plus side, he thinks 'we got better at utilising our local resources in recent years. BBC 5 Live is really good at partnerships.' But returning to the 2016 referendum, he concludes:

> I don't think I was ever asked how Lincolnshire would vote. But we were all doing our jobs, weren't we? There was a daily call between network editors and the TV regions, but that is always more about the mechanics of moving crews around the country and getting pictures. I can't think of a BBC forum in which I as a local radio editor would have been able to raise the issue or where I would have been asked. Building relationships has definitely fallen away over the years.

A senior executive at the time concurs: 'I understand that regional editors gave up feeding back what they were finding on the doorstep and in the pub because no one at the top took them seriously.'

So, there is work to be done. It remains murky how a science team based in Cardiff with a continuing brief to cover the whole of the UK will be stronger in influencing running orders drawn up in London. More broadly, we will know regional initiatives have succeeded when we hear that an executive in Salford has overruled a decision made in London, or if we wonder whether there's even a bias towards Scottish stories on the *Six O'Clock News*. The proposition is, after all, a simple one: London as one particular and unique part of the UK should not rule unchallenged over the rest of our diverse and fascinating land. Give power to the nations and regions and see what happens. It will, I reckon, be worth watching.

CHAPTER 9

DIVERSITY, DEFINITELY

When I was director of BBC London 2012, which remained logically as a London-based project, I visited parts of the capital I'd never even seen before. I got to know, a little at least, the Olympic boroughs of Newham, Hackney and Tower Hamlets. On planning trips to Hackney, host of our biggest music event in the run-up to the Games, I would take time out for coffee and people-watching in Mare Street, and for the weeks of the Games I lived in a rented flat in Tower Hamlets, which was within walking distance of the stadium in Stratford. These are among the most diverse parts of one of the world's most cosmopolitan cities, and they were quite a contrast to my own home borough of Richmond upon Thames, way out on the western extremity of the District Line. But I felt proud that this was also my city. A young and emphatically multiracial part of London was hosting athletes from all over the globe and an attempt was being made to create a legacy for boroughs which had long been neglected.

On the Tube journeys to and from east London I would muse about the challenge the BBC had set itself: we wanted the BBC's Olympics coverage to reach everyone in the UK. In a crowded carriage in the rush hour, I scanned the faces of my fellow passengers and saw the different generations and ethnicities with a multitude of life experiences – knowing we would have failed if they didn't find our content and didn't think the BBC was for them. It was a jab in the ribs about what universality means in public broadcasting: something for everyone, because they're the people who fund us. This was recognising that the Tube train, as it clattered along, was full of residents of London. Elsewhere in the UK there were the people working at Tesco in Orkney and the entrepreneurs of Birmingham and the hotel staff in Penzance, all of whom we needed to join the party. Viewing figures were only part of it – though in the end more than 51 million people saw the TV coverage and it was the most watched UK event of modern times – because we also polled regularly on whether audiences felt they were part of the Games. And they did. There was little evidence that anyone felt left out, and almost nobody criticised our tone or style as excluding age groups or minorities or viewers far from the capital.

I hope some of this was due to planning as well as to the star appeal of the Olympics. In the years before the Games, my project executive Amanda Farnsworth and I had travelled across the UK taking part in BBC staff meetings about what was in prospect – and we learned that we had to introduce London to some parts of the population in a manner that was as revelatory as for other Olympic host cities. Millions of UK citizens have never been to the capital. We sometimes used to say that London is as different from much of the country as New York City is from Middle America. Among the statistics we used: at that time, almost two thirds of all babies in London were born to parents who had started their lives outside the UK, and within the capital most of the countries taking part in the Games had a significant diaspora community who were now British residents. Stratford in London (40 per cent white) is not like Stratford in Warwickshire (97 per cent white).

What helped in bringing everyone together was Danny Boyle's opening ceremony. There had been a polite version of the culture wars which surfaced from time to time during the preparations. 'Celebrate the diversity of the host boroughs,' said some. 'Don't forget Britain's heroes in the wars of the twentieth century,' said others and usually whoever was Culture Secretary at the time. Danny's brilliance was in satisfying both camps. The Windrush generation of Caribbean immigrants were there, and so were the veterans from the Royal Hospital Chelsea marching alongside. The stadium fell silent for a moment to recognise the dead of the world wars, and it burst into life again with music from the culture of today. It was a Britain most of us felt we knew and could celebrate.

This is important because it provides a template for how diversity can be inspiring. There are more unsettling currents in which you're advised not to highlight ethnic minorities because it's 'political correctness gone mad' or not to delve into British history because it must mean the articulation of guilt and shame. Where many of the lobby groups go wrong is by starting from what you can't say rather than what you can. A focus on diversity doesn't eradicate the horrors of the past or the challenges of the present, but it can unify by identifying common ground on which we can gather.

That, I hope, is transferrable to news too – with some learning from 2012 still valid today. First, 'everyone' means everyone. Diversity is about the whole population of our islands. Second, London – as with many of the other themes in this book – really is different. Not all of the country has travelled at the same pace. Third, the culture wars are best resolved if there is no appetite to have winners and losers: it can be 'both/and' rather than 'either/or'. The country contains socially liberal atheists and religious conservatives, and there isn't much of an alternative to tolerant co-existence.

Public broadcasters generally get this. They have made a lot of progress in recent years in reflecting the changing UK. It is salutary to watch a programme junction or two from the 1990s, when Britain was already significantly multiracial, and to see every face in the shows and trailers being white. At the BBC, Tim Davie has rightly not seen any contradiction between advocating diversity in recruitment and on air while also arguing for rigorous impartiality on current controversies. Indeed, it is precisely because we are diverse as a country that inclusivity cannot mean excluding or disrespecting certain groups. The former director-general Mark Thompson made the argument for this breadth of approach when he spoke to the *New Statesman* in 2020: 'The BBC is more or less unique in constantly confronting its audiences with ideas, culture and lived experiences which are radically different from their own ... Like an NHS waiting room, you find yourself sitting next to all sorts.'

Over the years I worked with and sometimes mentored many BBC colleagues from ethnic minority backgrounds. I talked recently to the former correspondent Barnie Choudhury, now an academic and also editor at large for *Eastern Eye*, a UK-based south Asian newspaper, for his personal take on how the BBC is doing. He believes that the BBC 'tries really hard' on diversity and the top echelons of the corporation know what the problems are. But he notes that there is still 'anger' among more junior ethnic minority staff because not enough is being delivered, and he sees this partly as a consequence of middle managers who remain reluctant to recruit outside their own image. This echoes my own experience as a white, male observer. Too many candidates from minority backgrounds didn't make it to the level they should have, and there was an uncomfortable sense that there are glass ceilings in W1A. We should remember, too, that more than forty years after Margaret Thatcher became Prime Minister, no woman has yet served as director-general.

Yet the virtue of diversity, apart from it being right in principle, is that it makes output more interesting. Homogeneity and conformity are dull, whether in staffing or in programmes. Marcus Ryder, who has persistently argued for diversity, made the point to me that a wider recruitment strategy will also make for better editorial policy. Many of the decisions about impartiality are very finely balanced, but having people from a range of backgrounds can bolster confidence about getting it right. We should be honest that too many voices have been excluded in the past: not only people of colour but also many others because of geography or class or gender or religion or age. Aziz Rashid, like me a Bradfordian but in his case from a British Asian family, related a story about a BBC North editorial meeting he attended in which there was a discussion about Liverpool's plan to scrap free school uniforms. He asked the room if anyone else had received a free uniform in their schooldays – and nobody else had. 'For me,' he said, 'it had been a saviour: I got my school jacket, my trousers, socks, underwear – all from this scheme.' It is a reminder that the poor of all ethnicities are among those seldom heard.

I spoke to a reporter of colour within the BBC who believes that class even more than race is a dividing line:

The major programmes still look for a particular kind of external contributor, a person as I'd put it with a 'certain pedigree', and the producers are often all of a certain type too – quite posh, and many of them who knew each other from Oxbridge whatever their ethnicity. Not being like that, I have never really felt I fit in. I sometimes sit in editorial meetings and find them quite pompous and academic. There's not much connection with the bulk of our viewers and listeners.

Others are missing too. Of all the millions of Eastern Europeans who passed through Britain in the 2000s, how many were heard at any length on UK airwaves – even though they were paying their licence fees? Of those who have happily settled here, how many Polish or Romanian names do we now see on television captions? The former BBC News editor Marek Pruszewicz, himself from a Polish family longer established in Britain, sees a major gap:

> There has been nothing like enough done to widen representation of EU migrants and others from Eastern Europe. They still tend to feature only in stories about migration and the EU. I also feel the BBC has done too little to recruit from this demographic. Poles are the single biggest immigrant group in UK history. You would not be able to tell that from the BBC's on-air talent or senior management.

Pruszewicz gives an example of the treatment even he received within the corporation as a white, Oxford-educated man: 'The BBC remains the only employer where someone suggested to me changing my surname to something easier to pronounce. The request came when I first joined in 1992.' He rightly told the individual concerned to take a running jump.

Barnie Choudhury thinks that true internal diversity can also make for bolder reporting. He has no problem with putting contrary and sometimes offensive voices on the air, and he was responsible for some conspicuously brave reporting on the *Today* programme in the early 2000s. Based on a tip-off from the BBC Asian Network, he contributed a story on how parts of Oldham in Lancashire had effectively become no-go zones for white people, and he charted the rise of the extremist British National Party in northern towns. His journalism brought him death threats. He remains adamant:

> It is our job to challenge and interrogate, and you can't do that unless you put controversial people on the airwaves. There have been times when other people of colour have been highly critical of my role in doing that, but I am curious about why people think and behave as they do – and it is the BBC's role to give voice to all those who are able to contribute to the debate without fear or favour.

There is virtue in the cleansing properties of light. Leader of the BNP Nick Griffin shrivelled under the television glare of *Question Time*, and Choudhury's earlier reports prompted government initiatives to tackle racism and its causes. He wrote that the former Home Secretary David Blunkett told him: 'Barnie – we heard your reports and talked about them at Cabinet and acted upon them.'

This underlines the need not just for diversity but for diversity of thought – a willingness to challenge conventions, even if it is initially uncomfortable. It is why broadcasters need to make sure they recruit people from backgrounds which include, as a couple of examples, the socially conservative and the religiously observant. I do not have a faith myself, but I would put people who do in the category of the under-represented. This is not about the figureheads – an archbishop or an imam who can occasionally appear on a bulletin – but about ordinary Christians and Jews and Hindus and Sikhs and Muslims, who seldom get a chance to speak about their beliefs let alone see them positively represented in dramas or documentaries.

In the news reporting of the debate about abortion in America, which has riven that country for decades, opposition to abortion is almost invariably presented through the prism of a rouse-the-base right-wing agenda – without allowing for faith groups, notably evangelical Protestants and the Catholic Church, for whom the issue is a matter of moral teaching about the sanctity of life. Here, the BBC's now-departed LGBT correspondent Ben Hunte contributed an enlightening report on gay Muslims at the time of the Birmingham LGBT teaching dispute, which featured five interviewees, including one who identified as a 'gender non-binary queer Muslim'. It was excellent at showing the diversity within practising Muslims – except that I can't remember an equally prominent piece giving a platform to the views of conservative Muslims. That's diversity, too.

Probably the best remedy is to ditch the clichés about the way we see ourselves and others. This is tough for news desks that are up against time pressures and need the pictures and words that are going to fill the running order at 6 p.m. But try a personal thought for a moment. Do any of us see our lives and the places we live presented in a way we would applaud? As one of the more benign examples, I helped an ITV News film crew spend some time at the Cambridge college of which I'm head during the 2017 election. They talked to students and spent an hour or two filming them in the library, chatting in the café and walking round the Selwyn site. Normal things for normal young people. When the piece appeared on air, the student interviews were still there – but the visuals were all of punting on the River Cam, which some of them had never done, and the glory that is King's College Chapel, where many of them had never been. That, in telly terms, is Cambridge; the colleges which house most of the students from a multiplicity of backgrounds and the world-leading science labs never feature. Stereotyping of other regions of the UK can be more bothering. My home city of Bradford is routinely portrayed on television as poor and Asian, when it's actually majority white and in some areas prosperous, with a British Asian middle class which was thriving even in my childhood. But if they want to feature the middle class, the crew is already on its way to Guildford.

The diversity of the UK is, overall, becoming ever more of a mosaic. It is 67 million or more individuals, each with their own life stories. It no longer works to categorise broadly and simplistically. Where the broadcasters can up their game is by making sure staff recruitment recognises the complexity of the UK, and that there are no barriers to promotion and senior leadership. Then it is a matter of taking a different perspective from the hot air balloon: not just of the regions of these islands but of its peoples. It's far better not to prejudge who is right and who is wrong and to simply let them speak. What they say needs to be held to a standard of truth and accuracy, certainly, and kindness to each other should be encouraged, too. However, it is only by enabling these debates – which PSBs are best equipped to do – that we will find out exactly what being a diverse country means.

CHAPTER 10

EDITORS MUST EDIT

It's time to move from some of the foundations of a good newsroom – impartiality, diversity, respect for the nations and regions – to how they operate day to day. It is getting on for forty years since I first edited a news programme myself, and I wouldn't remotely pretend that I could cope with the changes in technology and working practices that have accelerated in recent years. But I keep in touch with some of the people who are editing now, and they are reassuring about how the basics of the job remain the same – and central to that are the editorial choices which dictate what we see, hear and read in the news.

This may sound like a statement of the staggeringly obvious, but there is no automatic way in which stories make it to the top of the running order. It is human beings who put them there. Each day there are thousands of things happening in the world that might be of interest, and only a very small number – a plane crash, a terror attack, a general election – are guaranteed to be broadcast come what may. There are a variety of routes to the airwaves for the rest: some items are picked from a planning diary of scheduled events; some will emerge from correspondents' conversations with newsmakers or a period of research that delivers a scoop; and others will end up on air for the worst reason – 'another channel is covering it, so we'd better not be accused of missing the story'. Diary items were seen by the more creative editors as the route to dreary programmes: 'Death by News Diary is what we used to call it,' says one. 'A list of anniversaries, press conferences, predetermined government announcements that could lazily be called the news. The challenge was always to be more surprising, more thoughtful about what actually mattered that day, not what you'd been told would matter by a planning producer.'

Some programmes, and therefore some editors, do literally set the agenda. The stories that the *Today* programme selects are usually followed up by later broadcasts, and on the Sunday morning TV talk shows, a few words from an interviewee, chosen by the producers in the hope that they will be newsworthy, can set a story running for days. At the time of the Birt revolution in the 1990s, some BBC news bulletins diverged wilfully and gloriously from the UK consensus – there was a deliberate attempt to seek the distinctive higher ground – whereas more recently there seems to have been greater homogeneity in the running orders across the BBC, ITV and Sky. But that is offset by the way newspapers remain vigorously partisan, often with radically different takes on the news agenda.

The role of the editor is most obvious in the world of print. Consider the *Sunday Times* under the great Harold Evans, or the influence of the *Daily Mail* under Paul Dacre or the ethos of *The Guardian* as it evolved under Peter Preston and then Alan Rusbridger and now Katharine Viner. I asked David Yelland, former editor of *The Sun*, for his take on the role of the editor, and he captured it with precision:

> When I was editing, my very famous boss said: 'All editors go mad: it is just a matter of how long it takes – a matter of time.' He was right, but it is also true that the job lies in the madness. All editors have obsessions, prejudices, idiosyncrasies, madnesses even – they go far too far or sometimes not far enough; they drive readers to action or up the wall. But it is in their individuality that the art of journalism rests.

If you have worked at the BBC or other organisations in the spotlight, you become familiar with one of the less attractive forms of this art when you are phoned by a press reporter seeking a story about you or your programme. Once you've explained the facts, there is sometimes the riposte, 'Actually, that's not the way the editor sees the story – what he really wants is…' which is the moment you know you are going to be skewered anyway, no matter where the truth sits. Editors have an uncomfortable amount of power in toying with the reputations of people who come into the public eye. In the past, there was scant attention paid to the human damage, as the phone-hacking episode showed most acutely. But it was newspaper editors who exposed the thalidomide scandal and pursued the killers of Stephen Lawrence, and it is editors who define the content that we read over breakfast or on the train to work. Without them, the news would be flavourless: no sense of priorities, no narrative that we can opt to share.

In broadcasting, editors are more hemmed in by the commitment to impartiality and the framework set by the regulators. But they still have a lot of power. The folk in charge of some of the flagships, especially those with a current affairs mission, can make waves: think of Esmé Wren's recent stint on *Newsnight* and Ben de Pear's award-winning incumbency at *Channel 4 News*. One of the charismatic editors I worked with was Jay Hunt, in charge of the BBC's *Six O'Clock News*, subsequently the chief creative officer at Channel 4 and now a senior leader at Apple. 'I've always thought the very best editors are passionate disruptors,' she told me recently.

They are affronted by the idea of groupthink and thrive by showcasing stories they think will excite and challenge the world. Editing a news programme isn't ever a vanity project, but I think it can occasionally be the distillation of a singular curious mind. And sometimes that's preferable to a sort of stultifying editing by consensus.

When I was editor of *Today* I would occasionally lunch with newspaper editors, and they were surprised by the amount of freedom we had. Their constraints were their proprietors and in some cases their advertisers, and an injudicious front-page splash could get them into bother, whereas on *Today* we almost never had any guidance from 'above'. I can't remember John Birt as DG or Tony Hall as director of news ever expressing an opinion on our choice of a programme lead, and my line manager Steve Mitchell was the model of non-interfering support. We therefore selected our 8.10 a.m. leads and our programme content ourselves, and one of the most important programmes in BBC News ploughed its own furrow – doubtless with some of the madnesses that Yelland defines within an editor's agenda.

The great broadcasting programmes owe much of their reputations to distinguished editors. *The World at One* was founded by William Hardcastle as presenter but also by Andrew Boyle as editor. I started on the *Today* programme under Julian Holland, a former features editor of the *Daily Mail* who could instil fear in his subordinates but had a kind heart. His editorial meetings, inspired by *The World at One* tradition, were gladiatorial combats in which if you were swiped by a sword, you had to swipe back to survive.

He disliked anniversary stories, beloved of other outlets: he thought they were lazy journalism, and when I see them I still recall Jules saying: 'Tell us if they mean something today, or don't bother.' He was followed as editor by Jenny Abramsky, another inspirational, driven editor who taught me such a lot. She would obsessively scan the agency wires – which chattered away in those days on teleprinters – and hurtle into the studio brandishing the breaking news. If, as the programme producer, I stuck with an older story, she would sigh in reproof: 'Roger, the programme is called *Today* – not "Yesterday".'

I was fortunate when I became an editor myself to have strong deputies and output editors working for me – they temper the obsessions of the boss and introduce new ones of their own. When I was head of television news, there was an amazing set of editors driving their programmes with Abramsky-type energy. The upside was that they produced engaging and varied content: there were days when the running orders of the *News at One*, *Six* and *Ten* were markedly different. There would sometimes be a radically different story choice, with different correspondents and different interviewees. But that points to the downside: it could be duplicatory – two crews doing the same story – and there were times when rivalries between programmes got in the way of focusing on the external competition. It was a BBC trait: the *Today* programme saw its rival as being the upstart 5 Live rather than commercial stations. This was understandably frowned upon by the top bosses, and various attempts were made, from cajoling to restructuring, to bring us into line – though many producers from those days would whisper that the programmes ended up better because of the internal competition.

It's here that we need to note the existence of two major forces that have driven television news. There was production – the people outputting the programmes – and there was newsgathering – the operation which employs the correspondents and deploys the crews. Newsgathering provided the 'core curriculum', the essential daily content for all programmes across television, radio and online. It has traditionally been more powerful at ITN, a simpler 'command and control' economy, than at the BBC, where programme editors would use it as they saw fit, sometimes supplementing it and occasionally not using it at all, to the frustration of the central planners. For all the time I was in television, production had the upper hand and saw themselves as the guarantors of creativity, but the urgency of the need for cost savings and an itch for more central control have recently tipped the balance decisively in favour of the newsgatherers. 'They have won,' one glum output editor told me during the 2021 reorganisation. Another noted that the newsgathering department was, with obvious pleasure, absorbing 'lots more money, resource and power'.

It is hard to chastise BBC News executives when they were faced with making savings of £80 million or more, and there is no question that much of what Newsgathering – newly rebranded as News Output – offers is good. The brave correspondents around the world and the health teams at home during the pandemic are Newsgathering employees. But there are consequences for audiences which are less appealing, with news increasingly 'branded and homogenised' in the words of one internal critic. Radio used to be much less reliant on newsgathering, and programmes such as *Today* and *The World at One* overwhelmingly generated their own content (radio has simpler logistics) and had their own reporting teams. Those have now all but disappeared. One of the reporters who chose to retire was the excellent Hugh Sykes, who explained it to me like this: 'There is now a new system of centralised commissioning of reporters for all outlets. This means that radio programme editors have lost their freedom to commission their own dedicated reporters to pursue original ideas and investigations. The result is often a tendency towards groupthink in story selection.' He believes there is a marked loss for the audience:

It means that on fiendishly complex topics – like the origins of coronavirus, the efficacy of vaccines and so on – instead of being analysed with carefully scripted reporter packages, they are tackled with live interviews, which are often clumsy and greatly depend on the guest being articulate. Previously, an editor might have said to me: 'Hugh, can you explain all this in a three-minute package and then we'll do an interview off the back of it.' Not any more.

So, the agenda has become narrower and the narrative has become coarser. Fewer people are feeding in to editorial decisions, which is a plus for efficiency but a minus for diversity of thought. An exclusive interview with the tennis player Novak Djokovic in February 2022 illustrated this very well. Novak speaks to the BBC: terrific! But it was plastered over every outlet: the major interview on *Today* at 8.10 a.m., a large chunk of the main TV bulletins, a special programme on BBC One that night and still playing on the BBC News channel days later. It felt like a disproportionate amount of airtime, especially for someone pushing an anti-vaccination message, even though poor Fergus Walsh as medical editor was deployed to run round after him saying: 'This isn't true.' I know this is heresy to the current generation of news managers, but I preferred it when some editors would like that kind of story and others wouldn't – and when they had a choice about the way they treated such a story, or even whether they ran it at all. That reflects not ill-discipline but editorial diversity. You can't claim to be against groupthink and then force the same thing onto every single platform.

The culling of independent-minded editorial posts is striking. A decade ago, there were separate editors for the

One O'Clock, *Six O'Clock* and *Ten O'Clock* television bulletins and different editors for individual time zones on the BBC News channel. Now there is just one output editor for all the main daytime and peak-time programmes. It would be easy to argue that there is a happy medium which has evaded the BBC: there used to be too many and now there are too few. Certainly, some of the veteran editors are unhappy. One, taking early retirement, used some of his leaving speech to lament the erosion of an editor's authority to choose what was in their programme. This would be fine if all audiences were the same, but they are not. As an example, the newsgathering machine delivered vast quantities of sport to Radio 4 during Euro 2020, often when a match was live on television – but Radio 4 is the place people are most likely to be taking refuge from the football. They would probably like to know more about Afghanistan and the pandemic instead. It would also be desirable if all central decisions were impeccably wise; they aren't always. The BBC was rightly criticised, at a crucial point in Russia displaying its aggression to Ukraine, when the *News at Ten* prioritised a set of dreary reports on the lifting of coronavirus restrictions in England. There are proven benefits in having empowered output editors who can pick apart a story and make it better or who can bring a viewpoint that's different to that of the planning team. Jay Hunt, as a conspicuously thoughtful former BBC News editor, draws this conclusion:

Cuts make innovating harder. There is no doubt about that. But if we all collectively sign up to a generic idea of what the news is we will end up bored to death by a humdrum account of our own world. And that should matter to society because a world we are bored by is a world from which we can all too easily disengage – with all the implications that has for democracy.

The outcome is therefore in the balance. News operations are becoming leaner at a time when we need them to reflect better a complicated, diffuse country – and when there is well-founded doubt about the centralising and concentration of power. I know from conversations with current senior BBC executives that they think I and others are barking up the wrong tree; they believe that the freedom to edit still exists if the right people choose to use it. But let there be no doubt: the model that has worked for generations has been disrupted, and traditional editors have been undermined. The BBC is trying to increase its range of voices while narrowing its editorial leadership. Letting editors edit still seems to me the best way to deliver creativity and spark to journalism.

CHAPTER 11

STICK WITH PRESENTERS

A funny lot, presenters. To the outside world, they're the stars of broadcasting on astronomical salaries. When you work with them, many are as riddled with insecurities as the rest of us – and probably more so because of the vulnerability that comes with a public profile. I am hugely fond of presenters, and indeed I'm a godfather to the children of two of them: Bill Turnbull and James Naughtie. But 'managing the talent' is never easy. During the height of the Gulf War, we sought to merge news and current affairs and their respective presenters into one set of BBC special events, and barely a night went by without a standoff about which distinguished presenter would be the first to be seen in the programme. 'If he does the introduction, I'm out of here' were words we heard more than once. Sometimes presenter traits are more amusing. In a mutual wooing session to get one presenter to the BBC, I was told that I had always been an inspiration to her. This flattery continued for as long as

I was her boss. But when she left for a better-paid job elsewhere, I wasn't even invited to her leaving party. Another presenter used to meet me socially for drinks when we were working together but didn't get in touch for some years after I had moved on. That was until the moment he realised I was in charge of the presenter rota for London 2012, when our friendship was suddenly resurrected with protestations of how maddening it was that we hadn't been able to get together for so long.

Presenters are an indispensable part of broadcasting, and yet their role is controversial. Only the briefest of mentions of presenters' pay and the internet starts bubbling away with indignation, while even the routine tasks of a presenter – such as reading the news – can be a matter of dispute. The great Jeremy Paxman has had newsreaders in his sights for quite a while: 'I can't see any point in reading the news at all,' he said on a podcast. 'Reading aloud, do you remember reading aloud at school? That's what it is. I don't think it has any grandeur or skill or anything to it. Any fool can do it.'

Other grand inquisitors have expressed the same view. Andrew Marr claimed in 2005 that newsreaders were paid too much money for merely reading a teleprompter, and John Humphrys chimed in saying that newsreading 'isn't work' and 'requires no brain'. I can testify that the newsreaders I know seethed in response, not least because both Paxman (on regional and breakfast television) and Humphrys (on the *Nine O'Clock News*) had spent their formative years reading from teleprompters. A colleague of both men murmured that teleprompters are not unknown on *University Challenge* or *Mastermind*. The truth is that long experience of presenting, even when it involves reading aloud, is what turns good presenters into excellent ones, and there are vanishingly few presenting roles which involve no journalism or interviewing or writing. The days are past when newsreaders were former announcers or actors, like Richard Baker or Kenneth Kendall.

The argument against the iconic modern presenter has been developed to question the very existence of the role. In a ruminative article in 2021, John Ryley, the head of Sky News, argued that 'the age of the all-powerful anchor is gone – instead they share the stage with journalists in the field'. When I talked to Ryley, he acknowledged that his views are shaped by his position at Sky:

> It might be slightly different if you're at the BBC or ITV. But what I was arguing was also that the grand generalists are fading out, and what we're looking at more is specialist journalism. I like to call it the era of the expert, in which you have journalists who really know their subject: Tom Clarke as our science editor, Beth Rigby on politics, Ed Conway on economics. They now help define Sky News.

His article informed a piece in *The Observer* by Vanessa Thorpe which baldly stated in its headline: 'Why the golden age of television presenters has had its day'. In the article Thorpe cited the views of one leading television news executive who had told her there was no point clinging to the old ways. 'Anchors do not work in the digital news world. And the really big interviews, like Emily Maitlis meeting Prince Andrew, don't come along very often.'

We shall leave hanging the question of how you get interviewers as skilled as Maitlis in her brilliant demolition of the prince if you don't give them the experience in the first place. But it is an opinion on presenters that I would say is wrong anyway: there is a counter-argument that says presenting talent is essential to differentiating yourself in the digital landscape and that known and trusted figures remain loved by audiences. Otherwise, it's just so much 'stuff' out there without any visible curation or identity. Ian McBride, formerly of Granada and ITV but now working for the American network NBC, notes that the emphasis in the United States is still around the major anchors: their Lester Holt is, he says, a 'calling card' for the network. Here in the UK, Adam Boulton – for many years political editor and presenter on Sky News – gave a valedictory interview to Times Radio in which he disputed the idea that the era of conventional television has passed: 'There is still life to be found in rolling news and having authoritative anchors.'

Those two things – rolling news and skilled presenters – go together. The strongest rebuff to the Paxman–Humphrys view of newsreading is that there are times when presenters are required to cope with breaking news, and someone equipped only to read out loud would be revealed as completely inadequate. Coping with a royal death or a ministerial resignation or a natural disaster is hard, especially when you have a stressed production gallery chattering away in your ears, and it is to the credit of news presenters that they usually make it look straightforward. Think of Reeta Chakrabarti on the BBC News channel in autumn 2021, when a crucial government announcement on new coronavirus restrictions was delayed by first one hour, then two, then three. She filled the airtime with aplomb, which is only possible if you have developed the skills over years of apprenticeship. Then there are the highest-profile programmes of all: the royal weddings and the general elections and the openings of Parliament and the state funerals and the commemorations for Remembrance Sunday at the Cenotaph. Britain is lucky to have the likes of Huw Edwards and Mishal Husain on the BBC; Tom Bradby and Julie Etchingham on ITV; and Dermot Murnaghan on Sky. We know what happens when that level of expertise is discarded: just remember how the coverage of the 2012 Jubilee River Pageant, designed to bring in new voices, ended up mired in the mud of the Thames.

The fact, too, is that some presenters have admirable editorial nous. I would sleep soundly as editor of *Today* if I knew that John Humphrys or Jim Naughtie was on the rota for the following morning, because they would devour the newspapers when they got into work at 4.30 a.m., and if anything had been missed by the overnight producers, they would demand action. There was nothing quite like Humphrys requiring a new running order at 5 a.m. I should say by way of balance that I have known other presenters with the journalistic instincts of a cheese sandwich, but the best of them provide an extra pair of editorial eyes and ears – and, most important, an instinct about the values of a programme. What works on *Channel 4 News* or on the *Breakfast* show on 5 Live will be different, but it is the presenters who front the programmes who can give producers a steer on running orders and the treatment of stories.

That said, presenters shouldn't have too much control. They must still work to editorial direction. One close observer says: 'Many presenters are being allowed to get too big for their boots. Some programmes risk being edited more by the presenters than by the editors.' And my former colleague at *Today* Hugh Sykes reminded me of the morning when a senior output editor took on an argumentative Brian Redhead. He wrote in mirror-writing on the glass window of the studio the instruction: 'Obey!' Given that presenters have often been the people who got the BBC into the hottest of water, it is worth reminding them who's in charge.

Getting the right presenters in place is more of an art than a science. Sometimes it can be completely instinctive. I had never thought of Nicky Campbell as a potential presenter for 5 Live until his agent brought him round to meet me, newly in-post as network controller, and yet it clicked into place almost instantly. A clever presenter from the youthful Radio 1 who wanted to move into speech radio: what was there not to like? Later on, 5 Live was struggling to find a new team for the *Breakfast* programme, trying to replace the irreplaceable Peter Allen and Jane Garvey, when a colleague suggested at the last moment that we should try adding the fresh voice of Victoria Derbyshire from BBC Radio Manchester to that of the unflappable Julian Worricker. It worked, but we had no idea whether it would until we nervously listened to them on air on their first morning.

By contrast, the move around of presenters on television in 2003 was much more informed by audience research and a long, collaborative process between television (managing director Jana Bennett and controller of BBC One Lorraine Heggessey) and my boss Richard Sambrook with me from the news division. We spent time talking to programme editors about their preferences, and then hours locked in an office doing the equivalent of a Cabinet reshuffle – contemplating a series of moves from a multiplicity of candidates and trying to work out who would fit best where. What is reassuring is how long it lasted. Huw Edwards was promoted to the *Ten O'Clock News*, along with Fiona Bruce for the weekend flagship bulletins. George Alagiah and Sophie Raworth became the faces of the weekday *Six*. We had no idea that the main parts of this settlement would endure for the best part of two decades, but it is a statement of the blindingly obvious that presenters have to be really, really good to stay at the top for that long.

What we were trying to do as broadcast executives was bring the next generation of presenters into the top roles – though we were also consciously placing them within a BBC tradition of authority and impartiality. With the occasional wobble, that has held. But it would be idle to pretend that there aren't now pressures in the other direction about engagement with the audience and revealing more personality. It's the insidious nature of social media that once you show a little bit of yourself, you risk being exposed more comprehensively. I am with Adam Boulton in his Times Radio interview when he spoke about the virtues of the greats such as David Frost and David Dimbleby. At their peak they were utterly commanding, and on air there was never a clue about their personal views. I doubt that either of them would have become Twitter warriors, and nor did they feel any urge to emote on air: the stories and facts would speak for themselves. Richard Sambrook is in favour of this traditional approach from all news journalists:

I do not like emotion. That was encouraged at one point to try to make items more accessible: warm hearted, human interest, easier to identify with and all the rest of it. It is not particularly good. There are all sorts of risks around

impartiality when you go down that line. I detect a slightly more sober tone returning to some parts of the BBC's
reporting, which I encourage because it is quite important
to have a more straightforward, factual, evidence-based
approach to reporting, from which there can be discussion and debate as well.

This absolutely does not mean, in my view, that generalist
presenters across the public broadcasters should be empty
shells with no opinions or passions. There is plenty of room
for the likes of Stacey Dooley and her award-winning documentaries, and in some radio formats – notably on LBC
– the success of Nick Ferrari and James O'Brien is based
on smashing the conventions of neutrality and bringing
personality to the fore. That is OK, and indeed sometimes
compelling, in the right place. But it will never be right for
the news flagships, where there has to be a quest for a narrative that can encompass everyone. Emotions attract, but
they also repel.

So, there will increasingly be a mixed market. More presenters will be hired for their views, but some will be required precisely because they do not express them. And it
brings us to the million-dollar, or at least the half-a-million-
pound, question: are any of them really worth the money
they get? I should confess here that now I'm outside the BBC
I'm sometimes phoned up by newspapers asking me to write

a piece about overpaid presenters. I always decline, not least because I have to admit I was sometimes part of the negotiations. I confess culpability. I was also a very well-paid employee myself, so I am doubly guilty. But let me have a bash at explaining why presenters are so handsomely paid.

The first is that there is a market. Commercial television and radio companies pay a lot of money for the right presenters, and what the BBC offers is often lower than the pay at external competitors. Then, as the former editor of *Today* Sarah Sands remarked: 'The BBC is built on the fault line between public service news and entertainment.' Huw Edwards and Fiona Bruce are defining figures for news on BBC One in a similar way to David Attenborough for natural history or Claudia Winkleman for entertainment. It is a perfectly legitimate question to ask why Edwards is worth £425,000 per annum, but it is equally fair to consider that he earns well under half the £1,130,000 a year paid to Zoe Ball for the Radio 2 *Breakfast Show*.

The BBC has, of course, recognised that some presenter pay did spiral out of control. That is why they have been persuading the top talent to reduce their salaries. But I have sympathy for the presenters who were given their deals after standard contractual negotiations with the BBC and were later portrayed in the papers as genteel versions of bank robbers. The responsibility for pay sits with the executives, not the talent. Who wouldn't shake the hand of a television boss who was brandishing a large cheque?

Having done those deals, though, I am in favour of making presenters work hard. It is a peculiarity of the British media compared with the American that on-air appearances are rationed: very few people work five-day weeks here. When I lived in the United States, I would wake up every morning to the same folk on NBC's *Today* programme, and it would be the familiar network anchors who presented the news seemingly every night, with their name still emblazoned in the title sequence even if it was a rare night off. It is still the pattern in most British radio, as evidenced by the explosion years ago when Chris Evans lobbied for the novelty of a four-day week on Radio 1. In UK television, it is not always sensible to insist on five-day weeks, because the working hours on unsocial programmes – *Breakfast* or the *Ten* or *Newsnight* – would be too crushing. A British presenter notes some pay differentials too:

> Yes, the American networks demand more in terms of days, but they pay handsomely for it too. Even Anderson Cooper on CNN is reported to earn $12 million a year, and Lester Holt is on $4 million. They invest in people in a way the BBC never does or can. US presenters are marketed and protected very carefully. Again, British broadcasting organisations are less good at this.

But trying to establish ownership of a programme remains important. After Paxman on *Newsnight*, the show fizzed best when Emily Maitlis, now departed, was having a decent run at it. *Woman's Hour* has been revived by Emma Barnett taking the leading role. By contrast, I am not alone in being perplexed by the randomness of the *Today* programme's rota. '*Today* is a presenting mess,' says one veteran broadcaster. 'Far too many voices and an absence of chemistry between them.'

It is only by working together most of the time – as John Timpson and Brian Redhead used to, or as Sue MacGregor, John Humphrys and Jim Naughtie did in my day – that a relationship is created for listeners. Presenters don't have to like each other, and indeed some of them hate each other's guts, but the best of them know how to spark off each other in a way that audiences enjoy.

My recipe, then, would be for fewer presenters overall, but to keep paying them well and also to maintain firm editorial control. When the online trolls say: 'I could do what they do,' I promise you that they couldn't, and it is ever more important that we are guided through the daily turmoil by people we can trust. A logo isn't enough: it needs the human touch, and we should nurture the calm authority that the best presenters can bring.

CHAPTER 12

DIVEST FROM POLITICAL PROCESS

When I applied to be editor of the *Today* programme deep back in the mists of time – 1993, in fact – I wrote a short manifesto for what I wanted to do with the programme. I had a reputation from *The World at One* of being a lover of domestic politics – which was true; we weren't nicknamed 'Westminster at One' for no reason – but I deliberately pitched my bid for *Today* as making the programme much broader than that:

> *Today* shouldn't be a specialist programme: its strength is range and diversity, and it should be seeking to broaden its agenda. The single most important task is to report Britain to itself. Government and society are becoming more complex: this must be reflected and explained by programme-makers. We should focus on the day-to-day concerns of our listeners in areas such as health, education, crime, the economy, Europe, science and leisure.

Reporting from the grassroots is vital in presenting the full picture.

It may not be the most surprising agenda, but we mostly delivered it. Reporters were recruited to be based in the northeast of England and in the Midlands, and the core team also spent a lot of time on the road. I particularly admired the late Sarah Cullen's revelatory pieces from the communities of Northern Ireland as the peace process struggled into life, which felt like they were opening a window into a foreign world. But I can't pretend that we didn't still obsess about Westminster politics too, and there was nothing wrong about that in principle. *Today* has a sophisticated, politically astute audience, and at its most noble we wanted to share what we knew was going on in Whitehall and the Houses of Parliament with intelligent listeners across the country. The industry liked what we did: we won Sony Gold Awards and were named radio programme of the year.

It therefore came as a bit of a surprise to find *Today* apparently under attack for its influence on the political process from one of the BBC's own correspondents, Steve Richards. In June 1994 he wrote a column for *The Independent* headlined: 'One brewed-up story, one headache: the media's hunger for political chit-chat gives John Major more trouble than any leader before him'. Richards analysed what had happened after a *Today* interview of Michael Howard, then Home Secretary, in which he had appeared to differ from the Prime Minister about a referendum on joining the euro currency. It had been followed by an alternative view on *The World This Weekend* from the Chancellor Kenneth Clarke, and within another forty-eight hours *Newsnight* was opening with a headline showing the front door of Downing Street with the stark question: 'Will John Major be out of Downing Street by the end of this week?'

Richards wrote at the time: 'The impression was of a government falling to pieces, but the issue was utterly artificial. If Mr Howard had not agreed to go on *Today*, or if the interviewer had focused on the economy, it would never have arisen.' At the time, I was pretty irritated that a BBC political correspondent was deconstructing the process in that way. After all, what he described was apparently what news programmes were there for: to get people on the airwaves and to tempt them into saying something interesting. Our belief that Europe would be the defining issue for the Tories was spot on.

But I would also admit that even at the time we were aware of what we were doing when we drummed up a political story on a quiet morning. I hope we didn't do this too often, but if we felt the urge to generate a headline or two, we would pop on air at 7.10 a.m. a Tory rebel – usually a Eurosceptic – saying that the government wasn't doing well and needed to get a grip. We would then call Downing Street to ask for a ministerial reply, and rather than castigating us for putting a backbench nobody on the air, they would frequently comply and offer us a Cabinet minister for 8.10. That would in turn make headlines on later bulletins and in the following day's newspapers, allowing us to count the number of times an interviewee was cited as 'speaking on the *Today* programme' and take satisfaction in the way we were setting the agenda. So, Richards was right to identify what was going on, and he had top-level support in doing so. The director-general of the time John Birt, who was never a fan of the short knockabout political interview, backed the thesis – again to our annoyance.

Richards went on to develop his critique later in the 1990s, when he wrote about the distorting focus on 'spin' and New Labour in parts of the BBC, which he believed came at the expense of scrutinising policy:

From the days of early New Labour, the BBC was obsessed with Alastair Campbell, Blair's press secretary. Fair enough. But a huge amount of genuine policy-making, for good and bad, was overlooked. I was at the BBC correspondents' office at Westminster at one point during this period when a senior political correspondent was berating 'spin' while waiting on the phone. Finally, he got an answer. 'Ah, Alastair…' He was berating spin while phoning to speak to the chief spin doctor.

Almost thirty years on, I wouldn't disagree with much that Richards wrote. What is depressing is that he believes 'it has all got much worse since then: more shallow, less depth. People at Millbank are unclear of their roles and purpose.' And I suspect that is true, too. There is no doubt that political editors and correspondents are resilient in the face of pressure from some pretty unsavoury operators, and the hysteria of Twitter users – from Corbynistas to Brexiteers with all points in between – makes the covering of politics ever more unpleasant. But my sense is that in the way modern politics seems broken, so does its reporting across all the channels – it's time for a rethink.

Let's briefly head to the United States to factor in what's happening there. James Fallows, the distinguished author and former speechwriter for Jimmy Carter, wrote an excellent piece in late 2021 which identified what makes political correspondents tick:

> The operational details of politics – the personalities, the dramas, the sausage-making, the grandeur – are part of what political reporters love about our work. We love knowing how the game is played, and recognising the parts of it that are game. We love being able to say 'what's really going on is...' or 'we're now seeing a big problem for the mid-term [elections]'.

He contrasts that with what the electorate care about, citing a public meeting with President Biden: 'The people at that town hall session, like most other people in most meetings with most candidates and officials, asked mainly about the *what* of government – education, vaccines, jobs, and so on. The press mainly asks the *how* of Biden's dealing with critics and supporters.'

Fallows called his piece: 'Politics-as-Sports: Why It Matters', with the subtitle 'Once you start noticing this "how-versus-what" pattern, you'll see it everywhere'. And you sure as heck see it emanating from the Millbank building near Parliament, which houses the political coverage of the major UK broadcasters.

Here's one example of how this manifests itself – not because it was the worst thing ever but because it illustrates the phenomenon particularly well. During the 2016 referendum campaign, Home Secretary Theresa May had been largely invisible. This was thought to be because she was an unenthusiastic supporter of the Remain campaign and was potentially keeping her powder dry for a leadership contest after the vote. It was therefore a coup to get her to sit down for a formal interview, and there was plenty to ask.

I am assuming here that that the electorate would have been most interested to hear her views about immigration and the wider case for staying in the EU. These were the defining issues for the biggest decision the country was going to make in decades, and in the three minutes fifty-five seconds of the interview that is still posted online, those questions were indeed asked. Mrs May said there was no 'silver bullet' to reduce immigration numbers. But she was challenged much more on issues of process. Had both sides in the debate put pressure on her to join them? Why had she been quiet during the campaign? Would David Cameron still be in office after the vote? And towards the end there was a brisk exchange: would May ever consider running to be Prime Minister? 'Would you rule it out?' – asked twice and followed up by: 'So you're not quite ruling it out?'

This is another case where there's plenty to unpick. First, May was not challenged in the same way about what she said on immigration when (a) she was the woman in charge and (b) this was the hottest topic of the campaign. Whichever side you take, it would have been interesting to know what the British government's options were. When she said there was no 'silver bullet' achieved by leaving, was that true?

Second, the process questions are largely pointless. There is only one answer that would really matter: 'Yes, Dave is toast and the TM for PM campaign begins now.' It is worth asking the question on the off chance that a political meteorite will strike. But in reality Theresa May was never going to say anything like that in a million years, and the 'Would you rule it out?' question is an obvious trick. If she says 'no', the political hares start running amok; if she says 'yes', it will be used against her when she does take part in a contest. As May correctly said in reply: 'Whatever I say to you is going to be taken this way or that' – and she could have added that at this stage voters cared about her career markedly less than they did about their national or European identity, their jobs and the future economy.

I will admit that this is the kind of interview I would quite likely have commissioned in my days as a radio editor, and what we see on our screens and hear on the radio today is still infected too much by this obsession with process. Much of political reporting is in a rut. This is not universal: I still find plenty to enjoy in the newspapers and magazines, where you can find helpful insights into the workings of Westminster. The likes of Stephen Bush, who spent seven years as political editor of the *New Statesman*, and Katy Balls in *The Spectator* are well worth reading; Tim Shipman has often been mandatory reading in the *Sunday Times*; and there are many more journalists doing a grand job. On television I'm often impressed by Nicholas Watt on *Newsnight* and Gary Gibbon on *Channel 4 News* – perhaps because they have the luxury of being slightly removed from the machine which generates round-the-clock content for all outlets.

But it is in the regular bulletins that the weaknesses are visible. Too many pieces start with the shouted question from the media pack to the Prime Minister when he emerges into Downing Street. A typical example from when the Downing Street party issue was running strongly: 'Is the party over, Prime Minister?' Everybody knows the question will never be answered. What it also represents is a question that cannot be answered sensibly but is instead what the media pack thinks will be amusing or set the agenda at the start of a report. Unless I've missed it, they have never shouted: 'What is your view on human rights abuses in China, Prime Minister?' or anything that actually matters. Worse still is an accompanying script line saying: 'The questions won't go away', when it's the media who choose to keep a particular line running.

During the pandemic, there were further revelations about the way the political pack operates. It now seems to be the law in broadcasting that ministers and officials can only be seen answering questions on the BBC from BBC reporters, on ITV from ITV reporters and so on. As the Downing Street health emergency briefings were broadcast live on the major networks, viewers across the country were able to see and be discomfited by the way news is made. I can understand that the pressures of deadlines – typically the briefings would happen after 5 p.m. with the bulletins due at 6 p.m. – meant that correspondents needed to 'drop in' key quotes from the news conferences to packages that had been prepared in advance. But the effect was still odd. No matter how interesting Boris Johnson's reply to the BBC, it was vanishingly unlikely to be used by ITV or Sky. Because Sky often came after the others, they would sometimes ask pretty much the same question again because they needed their correspondent to be seen asking it. 'I watched every night with my head in my hands,' says one distinguished former editor. 'You had to wait until the newspaper people asked their questions to get to any real journalism.'

This points to the wobbliness of some of the questioning. An early favourite, at its most basic, was 'How many people are going to die?' – to which the only answers could be, 'We don't know' or another attempt to explain how mitigations such as vaccinations were intended to reduce the toll. This question, like the virus, had some variants, often along the lines of 'How much worse could this get?' As we rolled up each year towards Christmas, the seasonal version was: 'Can you guarantee that we will be able to celebrate Christmas?' – which again had the only honest answer of 'We don't know' but was useful for the correspondents to store away and show how the government line had changed, if it subsequently did. From time to time political correspondents became epidemiologists, demanding the imposition or lifting of restrictions in line with the fashion of the day. To me, at least, it was a relief when the health, medical or science correspondents were covering the story instead.

This may sound like quite enough grumbling to be going on with, but there is more. Millbank is also unhelpful for diversity of thought. One reporter in a newsroom elsewhere notes that too many political correspondents have been of a certain type: 'Quite posh and white,' she says, though recent appointments at ITV have shown a readiness for change. The analysis from political correspondents sticks to the mainstream: their trusted sources seem to be the centre and right of the Labour Party and the centre and left (so far as it still exists) of the Conservative Party. So, analysis never tended to be sympathetic to Jeremy Corbyn, not least because the Parliamentary Labour Party had few genuine Corbyn fans. His strength was out in the country. In the same way, Iain Duncan Smith had a rougher ride in the 2000s than Kenneth Clarke would have done as Tory leader, because Duncan Smith was an odd-seeming Brexiteer from Essex while Clarke was a jolly man popular in the bars and smoking rooms. Their policies and grassroots support were as nothing compared with whether they were a hit with the media. So, it's not just the fascination among political correspondents about whether a leader is coping with party divisions and might even – joy untold! – face a challenge; it's also the lost opportunity to explore whether, for instance, Corbyn spoke for many voters on water or rail nationalisation or how much the Tory right were in harmony with English voters on the EU.

There are solutions to this. One might be less political coverage. The subject reviews launched by the BBC always recommended more of a particular topic, and I once sulkily drew up a list of the dozens of themes which we'd been encouraged to do more of in the flagship bulletins. At the time, only politics was officially approved as a subject that we might have over-covered; and that could well be right. We would not suffer if there were fewer interviews with backbenchers or even frontbenchers.

But it should also be possible to make the content from Westminster better by getting rid of the froth – the stuff that only matters within SW1 and which will be blown away by the next political wind – by focusing on the decisions the government and parliament are taking and what they mean for regular people. I asked a current practitioner about this move, and he replied that covering policy was undoubtedly better than process but 'hard to achieve'. That is too pessimistic. There may be a period in which correspondents and programmes have to readjust their news judgements, but they would be looking at stories about which the audience care more. Labour's policy on windfall taxes on energy companies is surely more interesting than the balance of power within the shadow Cabinet?

The risk otherwise is that we are in a vicious circle: democratic politics is fracturing across the Western world and media coverage reflects that – and makes the disconnection with the electorate even worse.

The American James Fallows, whom I cited earlier, is not just on the case now but spotted what was happening thirty years ago, at the same time Steve Richards was taking the BBC to task. Fallows wrote then: 'Step by step, mainstream journalism has fallen into the habit of portraying public life in America as a race to the bottom, in which one group of conniving, insincere politicians ceaselessly tries to outmanoeuvre another.' This, remember, was long before Trump and the rise of populists. And he went on:

> The press is often referred to as the Fourth Branch of Government, which means that it should provide the information we need so as to make sense of public problems. But far from making it easier to cope with public challenges, the media often make it harder. By choosing to present public life as a contest among scheming political leaders, all of whom the public should view with suspicion, the news media help bring about that very result.

There is a debate to be had about whether populist leaders are a product of this process or whether they show that the media was right to doubt politicians all along. But there has been a bad outcome, as Fallows predicted. The road ahead is either more of the same, with even worse consequences, or accepting the need for change. And there should be nobody better able to lead that attempt than the PSBs, not least because they have the most to lose if things turn even nastier.

CHAPTER 13

CHALLENGE THE POLITICAL NARRATIVE

There was a moment during one of the many brouhahas surrounding Boris Johnson when I was watching ITV's *News at Ten* and something unexpected happened. They had interviewed Paul Brand, their UK editor, for a view of the story, followed by political editor Robert Peston – who politely but unmistakably disagreed with something Brand had said. I'm told that this can make producers hold their heads in anguish. They expect, and we're used to, a common line. But why? Shouldn't correspondents sometimes disagree about a story?

What is odder, really, is the way that the conventional media – newspapers, radio and television – stick resolutely together on some stories, in a way that has made the term 'mainstream media' become something of a pejorative. An award-winning editor emailed me about one of the issues he worries about in political reporting and specifically about the Westminster lobby, which brings the media and politicians together in a regular, formalised way:

> The point, I think, is the way the lobby actively collaborates to create 'the line'. When I used to cover election press conferences, I was struck by the way the newspaper hacks and broadcasters all got together afterwards to agree – more or less – what interpretative line they would take. They were all terrified of their commissioning editors thinking they'd missed something, so it was better for them all to have the same news rather than risk any one of them saying something original and dropping the rest in the shit. This tendency homogenises political reporting and lowers its value.

I had a weirdly similar experience myself in the most unexpected place: the media briefing room at Everton Football Club on Merseyside. I was there in my sport management days and I'd been sitting alongside the commentators watching Everton take on Manchester United. Alex Ferguson was the manager of United, and he came along afterwards to talk to the assembled correspondents. It was, as you'd expect from Ferguson, plain-speaking, honest stuff. When he'd left, I was – perhaps naively – astonished by the way the journalists operated. They methodically agreed which quotes they would use and what would be left out (one or two of the fruitier bits), and then they carved up the parts of the story that would be used for the Sunday papers and what would be left as fresh quotes for Monday. I remember saying to people at the time: 'It's just like the Westminster lobby.' I completely see why it suits the media pack to operate in this way: the manager can talk freely knowing that any indiscretions will be softened, and the papers get their story. But it is largely the same story.

Some of the overt collusion at Westminster has changed. Robert Peston recalled in a lecture the way it was in the lobby in the 1990s:

> Late afternoon every day the political editors of what were then known as the 'white' newspapers would go into a huddle to agree the latest attack line against [John] Major. I was political editor of the pink 'un, the *FT*, and sanctimoniously stood to one side. The press was a galloping herd that destroyed Major under its hooves.

He brought the story up to date:

> An important question is whether the continued existence of a cadre of political lobby journalists – endowed with privileges by Parliament, living cheek by jowl with each other in a rook's nest at the top of the Palace of Westminster – helps or hinders trust in the media, in this era of institutional mistrust. To be clear, there is no longer

explicit collusion between hacks, and there is much less hole-and-corner secrecy.

But the proximity within one tiny part of one small postcode is a problem, I reckon. Some of this is driven by logistics. Parliament is a village. The media pack, in non-pandemic times at least, literally travels as a pack: they are accommodated on the buses and trains and planes that take politicians and royalty across the country and around the world. There is an expectation on long-haul flights that the principal characters will sometimes wander down the plane to have a chat, and many a story – good and bad – has emerged from a 747 flying through the night. This can be enlightening, and access is good. But what is bothering is when the pack operates together even when its members are physically separate, and where there is a unified view on some of the big issues facing us. Groupthink remains a real and present danger.

This is seen at its most vivid when the pack, and editors, have decided there is one story that matters more than anything else. It is obsessed about it to the exclusion of the rest of the world. The pursuit of Boris Johnson over parties was a classic example – a story that was completely legitimate and important in that his career depended on the outcome, but one in which the media added fuel to the fire while pretending they were simply observing. For a start, any gathering was automatically deemed to be a party. Some were – the garden drinks in Downing Street on 20 May 2020 – and some weren't. But so anxious was everyone to make the story trend in the same direction that there was no room for nuance. The Prime Minister was interrogated at length in a pooled interview about a party he hadn't been at on the night before Prince Philip's funeral. The language was emotionally charged, with a reference to the Queen and 'the night before she laid her husband of seventy years to rest'. Johnson appeared defeated and humiliated on camera – because of his political sins, but also because the interview was constructed to be only about his personal defeat and humiliation. Ross Clark broke free from the narrative to write in *The Spectator*:

> There must come a time when even Beth Rigby [of Sky News] starts to ask whether she is too fixated on a small staff party which happened nearly two years ago and not quite enough on the highest inflation rate in thirty years and the prospect of a Russian invasion of Ukraine.

That's one view of perspective, and another came on the same day from Alexander von Schönburg, correspondent for the newspaper *Bild*, in a piece for *The Times* about the German view of Johnson's travails:

> We were astonished by how blatantly he circumvented constitutional convention when he prorogued parliament to stifle resistance to his Brexit manoeuvres. We were

shocked when he threatened to override the exit deal he had signed with the EU because details concerning the sea border with Northern Ireland were no longer to his liking. So the fact that his downfall could come about from attending an outdoor drinks party seems a little out of proportion.

This was a line that was only allowed to be used by pro-Johnson interviewees. Political correspondents instead unanimously insisted on two things. The attention, they said, had not moved away from the parties. As usual, this was because they had chosen not to move attention from the parties, which for a long time they all thought more interesting than Ukraine. Quentin Letts wrote a sketch for *The Times* about this phenomenon during the PM's visit to India:

The PM was keen to publicise £1 billion worth of deals his India trip clinched, supporting thousands of new British jobs. A green push. Offshore wind developments. Helicopters. Electrification of Indian public transport. Undersea capabilities in the Indo-Pacific. A 'UK–India 2030 Roadmap'. Engines for Indian fighter jets. All this and more.

The London journos: yeah, but what about the birthday cake?

Those journos then put all government policies through

the prism of the party controversy, so everything from the end of Plan B Covid restrictions to the BBC licence fee was seen as a Johnson comeback attempt. There is, of course, undoubted truth in this; but it's also the case that the government was damned if it did and damned if it didn't – if it announced policies, it was bad, but if it didn't announce policies, it would be condemned as rudderless.

The reporting of general election campaigns has been a long-running example of the dangerous power of the narrative. There were certainly people who got it right on each occasion, but in the UK in 2015 there was a widespread media assumption that the outcome would most likely be a hung parliament, similar to the result in 2010. In 2017, there was a belief that Theresa May would get something close to a landslide. One newspaper was far from being an outlier with its headline on polling day: 'Theresa May will win biggest Tory landslide since Thatcher, final survey predicts'. In 2019, the outcome was portrayed as likely to be close – with much less talk of a thumping Tory majority, which happened, than in 2017, when it didn't. We saw something similar in the United States in 2016. It was a 'Madam President' edition that *Newsweek* inadvertently circulated (125,000 copies were reportedly sent out) before the outcome was known, with a pre-prepared explanation of her victory: 'President-elect Hillary Clinton "went high" when her opponent and his supporters went ever lower … On election day, Americans across the country roundly rejected the kind of fear and hate-based conservatism peddled by Donald Trump.'

All journalists have prepared material that turns out to be useless when events change, but on election night 2016 I was glued to the NBC and CNN special coverage as they waited for the polls to close. It was nailed on that Clinton was going to win. All the polling evidence cited by the networks pointed to a comfortable Democratic victory; American political pundits, whom I'd up to then have trusted with my life, assured viewers that it was in the bag for Clinton; and I dropped off to sleep on the sofa comfortable that I knew the outcome. It's the only time in my life that I can say I woke up to a nightmare.

This does matter. It makes you wonder what aspects of the political consensus are also wrong but less noticeable, and it distorts campaigns in a way that can be deeply unfair. The narrative of a likely hung parliament in 2015 had two serious consequences. First, it meant that Ed Miliband as Labour leader was hounded for much of the time by questions about whether he would form a coalition with the Scottish National Party. The people who shout at politicians in Downing Street were on the road, shouting this time about pacts between Miliband and Nicola Sturgeon. Looking back, it took Labour a little time to spot the danger of the political attack, but when they did it was hard to pick it apart. This, for instance, is what the shadow Chancellor Ed Balls said a week before polling day: 'The SNP have said they don't want a coalition. It's not part of our plans. We don't want one, we don't need one, we're not after one … It's the last thing we want. What we want is a majority Labour government.'

Yet Labour leaders were challenged on programme after programme, and horserace hypotheticals were deemed to be vastly more interesting than policy proposals. This was particularly problematic because the alleged threat of a Labour–SNP coalition was part of the Conservatives' agenda. Remember how often Prime Minister David Cameron said the choice before the country was simple? This was a sample tweet: 'Britain faces a simple and inescapable choice – stability and strong government with me, or chaos with Ed Miliband.' The idea of a coalition of chaos, even involving Sinn Féin, was a Tory staple.

Relatively unexamined was what a majority Conservative government would mean. In particular, there has been speculation that Cameron assumed the pledge of an in–out referendum on the EU was unlikely to happen because he'd be in coalition again with the Liberal Democrats. But it was there in black and white in the manifesto, and there was nothing to stop the media fixers shouting questions at Cameron about whether he really thought offering the chance to quit was a responsible option. Instead, it was back to Labour's coalition plans.

A few months after the election, BBC political editor Laura Kuenssberg wrote an excellent blog about what had gone awry – particularly in the opinion polling:

The dozens of surveys carried out by a host of polling companies did, to a significant extent, frame the discussion of politics, the examinations of policy, and the questions that politicians were asked by journalists like me … Yesterday, one Conservative minister privately marvelled at how effective their party's attack line was, asking voters to imagine a coalition between the SNP and Labour under Ed Miliband.

In other words, it was a choice – albeit a choice influenced by what was believed to be polling 'evidence' – that the media went down the line they did. You will spot the pattern emerging when we look at 2017 and see that it all went terribly wrong again for the media. It's less clear whether the widely shared and incorrect narrative of a Tory landslide had an effect on the result, though some believe the late increase in Labour's vote was because we were repeatedly told they couldn't win and it was therefore safe to cast a protest vote for Jeremy Corbyn. But the media found themselves chastised again, with this typical comment in the industry's *Press Gazette*: 'As results poured in on Thursday night, political commentators were left wondering why they had spent their weeks arguing about the size of Theresa May's majority, instead of asking themselves if she would have one at all.' Two quotes from the piece stand out. First from the columnist John Rentoul, who said: 'Commentators ought to try to convey uncertainty, but it's human nature. Readers want to know, they don't want to be told that no one has any idea what will happen.' Second from *The Guardian*'s John Harris, who made a specialism of travelling the country and talking to the public:

> I knew something was shifting when I went to Wolverhampton ten days before polling, and met several people who had really warmed to Corbyn and Labour in the course of the campaign. Similarly, it wasn't hard to detect the momentum behind the Leave campaign in 2016 by going out in the country and talking to voters. The lesson: root more reporting in the real world.

Yet still in 2019 there was a collective inability to frame the campaign properly, and one seasoned observer thinks part of that was the recognition that the media had got it wrong so badly in the past on Brexit and Trump and more. Editors were, he said, 'fearful' to call anything given those past mistakes.

So, there can be a clear prescription here. Yes, I repeat the endorsement for more reporting from the ground but also for having the courage of your convictions. If you see it with your own eyes and hear it with your own ears, you can break free from the pack. Then, in delivering the national coverage: try to give the best picture you can of what's happening, but keep testing yourself before you allow a single narrative to take hold.

There is always an evidence-based scale of likely outcomes: in 2015 there were multiple possible outcomes with no party likely to have a big majority, while in 2017 and 2019 the range was from a Tory landslide to a hung parliament. Nobody was seriously going to contest your impartiality if you didn't invest much airtime in the idea of the Lib Dems or even Labour forming a majority government in 2019. But also, and this remains crucial too, keep prodding the hypotheses and do not become obsessed with a single scenario. In the end, parliamentary arithmetic will decide who forms the government, but an individual voter in a constituency is far better taking a decision on what they believe than on what that mathematics might be. By now, they should be rightly sceptical of the media telling them what's going to happen.

CHAPTER 14

BRING BACK THE GRID

Like most journalists, I was irritated by regulators. Our job was to get out the news as best we could, trying to be as fair as possible, and it was dispiriting to be summoned before an internal or external panel some weeks later to explain yourself. I once had to appear before a sub-committee of BBC governors to defend Kirsty Wark for a section of *Newsnight Review* in which she was alleged not to have challenged sufficiently an extreme remark by a guest. I made the obvious point that in live programming it is sometimes hard to cope with the unexpected, and a presenter cannot guarantee to handle everything with perfection. The governors then chuntered on for half an hour or more about what Kirsty should have said – thus making the point much better than I could. They weren't sure after thirty minutes' discussion what her response should have been, and yet they were sitting in judgement on a decision she had made in a split second. And if we had our doubts about the BBC governors, they were multiplied ten times by the ineffectual BBC Trust which replaced them. An afternoon with one of their committees made executives, or me at least, yearn for an alternative lifestyle running a teashop in Whitby.

On programmes and in big departments such as Television News, we were equally resentful of interference, as we saw it, by senior management. They generally let us be, but inevitably there is a hierarchy at the BBC and it is certainly true that the very top executives might carry the can if we got something wrong. The *Today* programme's scoop on the government's documents about the Iraq War in 2003 brought down the director-general and the chairman. It was therefore legitimate for the executives to keep an eye on what we were up to and to set objectives for the corporation's journalism.

At which point, The Grid makes its appearance. There were, in fact, multiple grids, and they were charts about major events which attempted to work out who was doing what and when. They were beloved of Mark Byford when he was deputy director-general and head of journalism, with a role which he describes as: 'I ran nothing, but I was responsible for the lot.' The most important grids were rolled out for general elections, when they would plot the days and programmes on which leaders would be interviewed, along with the issues that must be covered by output areas. So, in 2005 we knew the slots in which Tony Blair and Michael Howard and Charles Kennedy would be interviewed, and we also committed that the *Today* programme would cover foreign policy, for example, in a structured way, while there would be a package on the television news bulletins about the parties' proposals on agriculture, along with other areas of their manifestos.

Reader, I hated the grids. My output editors did too, and we may even have called them anti-journalism. In early iterations of the grid, when I was editor of *The World at One*, I would drive along the Westway into work listening to the *Today* programme and grinning happily because they were stuck with their dutiful grid items, leaving all the actual news of the day and the key interviews to be swept up by us. What we wanted to do was cover the campaign trail and all the ups and downs of the parties' pitches to the electorate, whether it was the story of Jennifer's Ear (all-consuming in 1992; largely forgotten now) or Tony Blair and Gordon Brown awkwardly eating ice cream together or commentators debating the Tories' dodgy dog-whistle advertising campaign. We didn't care about agriculture policy or housing, and we broadcast the pieces only because the grid told us we had to.

We were, of course, wrong. The 2016 referendum and the general election campaigns of 2015, 2017 and 2019 showed precisely why you need a grid to give the right issues some traction and avoid the agenda being driven by the spin doctors and the Westminster pack. Byford was clear: 'Parties do not set our agenda. We set our agenda.' There will inevitably be tension, sometimes acute, between what the broadcasters want to do and what the parties prefer to talk about, but the broadcasters need at least to put up a fight and not be driven by the press releases of the day.

One of Byford's other initiatives was more popular at the time. He ran a project titled 'Big Stories', which aimed to identify what the biggest stories of the year were likely to be and then to plan their coverage. He told me what his aims were:

The BBC is supposed to be about the best journalism in the world, and I wanted to define what that meant. How to be ambitious, distinctive, revealing – and getting a wide range of views and depth of commitment through the year. So typically we might identify five or six big stories – though I remember in 2007 there were nine – and they might be about the economy or China or climate change. And we would bring in experts to brief the senior editors; we would commission audience research about what viewers and listeners knew already, and what they wanted to learn more about; and I would cajole and try to inspire and monitor how we were doing in getting on air the best reporting and – also crucial – the widest possible range of viewpoints.

This was a commitment across BBC News, from the World Service through to English local radio. Byford concedes that it didn't always deliver – 'Sometimes it worked; sometimes the themes got lost' – but I can say from experience that the briefings and research were enormously helpful, and it is simply right to commit to covering phenomena such as Putin's Russia or the rise of modern China in a systematic way. This is because these countries are hard to read and usually generate few on-the-day headlines – but we now know just how much the deliberations going on there affect us all. Better planning can shape the more obvious lead stories, too. The US presidential election in 2020 was covered as a horserace between Trump and Biden, but some of the veteran hacks believe there wasn't enough analysis of what a Biden administration might mean – in economic policy or foreign affairs – because Trump's antics were allowed to overshadow the deeper differences between the candidates.

Another intervention in the journalism about which I was wrongly sceptical was the launching of subject reviews by the BBC governors and then by the trust. The idea was to get external experts to examine the reporting of controversial topics – the Israeli–Palestinian conflict was an early choice – and publish their reports. This initially felt like too much outsourcing of core editorial business, but in practice it worked. In particular, recommendations on reporting of the UK nations brought significant and overdue change to an operation that had been too Anglocentric. There was the inevitable outcome that every review wanted more coverage of the subject it was reviewing while programme durations remained finite, and every review tried to call for a dedicated editor in its subject, which came a cropper in Religion – it is hard to imagine a dodgier appointment to that role than Martin Bashir – and elsewhere. But the absence of these reviews in the early years of the BBC's integrated board has been felt, and it was another welcome aspect of the Serota review of impartiality in 2021 that it called for their return: 'Previously, the BBC commissioned reports into how it covered specific subject areas such as science or immigration. Reintroducing similar thematic reviews would enable the board to monitor whether the BBC has the desired level of coverage in particular areas and an appropriate breadth of voice.'

My former boss and director of BBC News Richard Sambrook applauded this in a committee appearance at the House of Lords at the end of 2021. 'Having experts in various fields who lead those reviews from outside the organisation is very valuable ... The key thing is to break down some objectives, measure performance against them, decide which are the key ones to test and get some external review in. It definitely makes a difference.'

He's right. In the maelstrom of daily news, the addition of structures and long-term plans – especially if they involve dragging yourself off to yet another corporate meeting – seem like the last thing that you need. But accountability and challenge are vital. Bring back the grid!

CHAPTER 15

INVEST IN INTERVIEWING

It is a justified criticism of broadcast journalism that it doesn't get scoops in the same way as newspapers and websites. There are two probable reasons for that. First, it is easier to write a story than it is to deliver it as a polished piece of broadcasting. A smart journalist with a computer and a phone can come up with some powerful revelations in 1,000 words online that wouldn't immediately translate into a two-minute, fifteen-second package with moving pictures for the evening news. Second, the risk appetite of broadcasters is lower. They are officially regulated, and they have higher thresholds for editorial approval of stories. Sometimes this is ascribed to over-cautious managers, and there may be some validity in that. I can testify that there were times when I thought a contentious story was almost certainly true and of public interest and I would have loved to run it, but I could also see that the 'almost' was a problem and the reputational damage to the BBC of getting it wrong would have been enormous.

Where the broadcasters do score day after day with exclusives that make the news is in their interviews. It is particularly the case with radio, where LBC or Radio 4 or 5 Live without interviews would bring the national agenda shuddering to a halt. This is an area in which the broadcasters are doing a valiant job, but the malign forces of politics and spin are conspiring against them, and we need to preserve the characteristics which make interviews of most value. At their best, they can give unique insights into policies and personalities; they illuminate and persuade. At their worst, they're a scrappy fight between two jaded people which leaves the audience jaded too.

When you see an interview done by a skilled operator, it's riveting. I had missed it at the time of transmission, but viewing a showreel for the 2022 Royal Television Society Journalism Awards I was full of admiration for an interview with President Museveni of Uganda by Channel 4's Lindsey Hilsum. It was challenging, but we could listen to Museveni and make our own assessments of his case for re-election. She put him on the spot about shootings by security forces in his country in which fifty people had lost their lives. 'Who was responsible for that?' she asked. 'The opposition,' he replied. 'So victims are responsible?' countered Hilsum, citing the death of a fourteen-year-old. Later, she wondered whether, after thirty-three years in power, Museveni still saw himself as a freedom fighter. 'Yes,' he said, but added: 'You are very superficial.' 'I'm a very superficial person, you're right, Sir,' she said and ploughed politely on with her questions.

What was revelatory was not just the content but Museveni's demeanour. He took that little bit of lip from Hilsum in his stride when others might have stomped out of the interview. And that is the joy and terror of interviewing: you never quite know where it's going to get you. It is an enterprise in which presenters and producers come together to get the programme on air and try to make some news, though it's the presenters who are in the spotlight while we are the ones chewing our nails in the control room.

There are important stages before that happens. The first is that interviews need to be arranged, and this can involve many months of wooing – as for Prince Andrew's ill-fated encounter with a brilliant Emily Maitlis. Or it can involve sweet-talking whoever's in the news on the day and trying to get them on your programme. On Radio 4 programmes, we prided ourselves on persuading newsmakers to appear on our airwaves and reject all the other requests they were receiving, especially if they were from the ghastly lot in television. The second is that there is an interview planning process, if time and resources allow. The terms are agreed with the contributor – what's the format? What's the key thing you want to say? – and then the item producer will offer a briefing to the presenter.

Sometimes this can be very brief indeed, and on the

hoof. Some of the *Today* programme's 8.10 interviews were 'planned' by John Humphrys and me yammering at each other while the 8 a.m. news was being read. 'If he says A, you should ask B, but if he won't answer that then you need to take Option C' might have been one of our more structured conversations, with 'let's just bloody nail him' the occasional fallback. Ideally, and certainly for the more major interviews, there is a collating of background information to make sure of the facts and a testing of what lines of questioning will be most productive.

Even so, there is a scary amount of uncertainty. Before a lengthy special Tony Blair interview in 2003, Jeremy Paxman and his editor George Entwistle and I spent a few minutes kicking around last-minute thoughts. The Iraq War was looming, and Blair's relationship with George Bush would define him. 'Shall we ask whether they've ever prayed together for guidance?' we mused. Surely the Christian Blair and the evangelical Bush might do that? 'Too cheesy,' we all agreed. But it happened. It is an example of an opportunity popping up within an interview and also of a pitch-perfect response from the Prime Minister, who killed it stone-dead. The episode was remembered for the question, not the answer.

Paxman: 'I want to explore a little further about your personal feelings about this war. Does the fact that George Bush and you are both Christians make it easier for you to view these conflicts in terms of good and evil?'

Blair: 'I don't think so, no. I think that whether you're a Christian or you're not a Christian you can try to perceive what is good and what is evil.'

Paxman: 'You don't pray together, for example?'

Blair: 'No, we don't pray together, Jeremy, no.'

Paxman: 'Why do you smile?'

Blair: 'Because – why do you ask me the question?'

Paxman: 'Because I'm trying to find out how you feel about it.'

Blair: 'Possibly.'

Isn't that 'possibly' brilliant? And Blair's tone, if you watch the recording still available on YouTube, combined humour and a flash of irritation, but he made the studio audience laugh in what was otherwise a grim programme about an impending war. He was, at his peak, the finest media performer.

Other celebrated questions had more planning. In the 2017 general election campaign, ITV's Julie Etchingham asked Theresa May in a sit-down interview, 'What's the naughtiest thing you ever did?' and was rewarded by this response:

Oh, goodness me. Well, I suppose – gosh. Do you know, I'm not quite sure. Nobody is ever perfectly behaved, are they? I mean, you know, I have to confess, when me and my friend, sort of, used to run through the fields of wheat, the farmers weren't too pleased about that.

When I talked to Etchingham, she told me that the idea had come to her in the preparations for the interview because she had become intrigued by May's persona: the ultimate introvert in a Westminster world of extroverts. She was struck by the Prime Minister's background as the daughter of a vicar and the loss of both her parents at a relatively young age:

> I felt she was very much shaped by her background. She'd been a dutiful, conscientious daughter and had carried that sense of careful duty into adulthood – and I was genuinely curious about whether she ever had been naughty in the conventional way, which is why I planned to ask that question.

After she left office, May said that answering the question was 'the silliest thing I ever did'. I'm not sure: it was honest, and the problem was more with her political rivals and the media going giddy about something they found a laugh. If, however briefly, a human side is revealed, that is part of the assessment that voters make of politicians. Etchingham regrets that the sections of her interview about policy – including a lengthy discussion about free school meals – were overlooked in light of the wheat field sensation. She has an aversion to 'gotcha!' moments, and I agree with her that the 'naughtiness' question isn't that. But May also came a cropper when she refused to answer a perfectly reasonable question put to her by LBC's Iain Dale. In an interview in the autumn of 2017, while the Brexit negotiations were still grinding on, Dale asked her: if there was a new referendum on membership of the EU, how would she vote? Despite five attempts from Dale, she simply declined to answer whether she would be Remain or Leave, and thus earned herself days of lacerating headlines because she was unable to express a view on what she insisted was a hypothetical question.

Dale told me he sees reasons for optimism about the art of interviewing:

The long-form interview is making a comeback, and about time too. A calm, softly-softly approach often gets far more out of someone than when in a short interview the interviewer goes in all guns blazing right from the off. The politician's defences go up and they fall back on pre-prepared soundbites, and the viewer or listener is the ultimate loser.

Certainly, the most revealing moments are from long and robust interrogations of our national leaders. That is something we have expected since television and radio came of age, and in my youth I would be on the edge of the sofa watching Robin Day battling with the statesmen and occasional stateswomen of the day. The party leaders – Wilson and Callaghan, Heath and Thatcher – would submit themselves to interviews in the peak BBC One and ITV schedules, and it was seen as part of the accountability of the Prime Minister. ITV added the Sunday programme *Weekend World* to its schedule in 1972, which – under Peter Jay and then Brian Walden – developed into one of the most intellectually rigorous of forums for politicians to explain their policies. Set-piece political interviews were still special events, and they absolutely didn't happen day in, day out. When I started working in national broadcasting myself, even an interview with the Chancellor of the Exchequer was a rare thing. It would be thought of as a scoop if Nigel Lawson agreed to come on the programme. Interviews with the Chancellor were forbidden in the run-up to a Budget or public spending statement, with official 'purdah' in operation, which kept him hidden away in Whitehall to protect his secrets. As late as 1992, Norman Lamont was reappointed as Chancellor after the April general election but didn't give his first interview – to *The World This Weekend*, which I was editing – until just before the summer parliamentary recess.

That changed in a puff of cigar smoke when Kenneth Clarke became Chancellor. We put in what we thought was a hopeless bid for him to come on the *Today* programme just before the Budget, and he cheerily rolled up and at least set the context for his announcements. Nowadays, Chancellors spill the beans about almost everything. Larry Elliott wrote in *The Guardian* in 2021: 'These days there is no such thing as Budget purdah, merely Budget news management and Budget spin. Parts of the statement are selectively trailed, sometimes in the form of leaks to government-supporting newspapers, but more usually through press releases, in the days leading up to the statement.'

He could have added, or by Rishi Sunak perching on the sofa on the *Andrew Marr Show* on the Sunday before his Budget and lobbing in an extra story or two for the Monday papers. And this is just one example of an unwelcome outcome: politicians seem more available than ever but are in reality less accountable. They seek to set their own terms for broadcasts, and interviews are seen as part of a daily communications grid, far away from the idea that the public have a right to know about – and judge – their actions through a long-form examination. If they don't fancy being interviewed, they can tweet.

What has happened in parallel is an industrialisation of the interviewing system. It used to be that a guest was booked by an individual programme, but now the multiplicity of outlets and the spin doctors' urge for control mean that one politician can be deployed across a dozen outlets or more in one day. The estimable Politico daily newsletter tells you who's going where, as in this typical example from early 2022:

Health Minister Ed Argar broadcast round: Sky News 7.05 a.m., Times Radio 7.20 a.m., *BBC Breakfast* 7.30 a.m., LBC 7.50 a.m., *Today* programme 8.10 a.m., TalkRadio 8.50 a.m.

Shadow Climate Change Secretary Ed Miliband broadcast round: *Today* programme 7.10 a.m., *BBC Breakfast*
7.20 a.m., Sky News 8.05 a.m., LBC 8.20 a.m., Times Radio
8.35 a.m.

Now, it has been the case for ever and a day that parties try
to control the news agenda. When Bernard Ingham was
press secretary in Downing Street, his version of it was to
ban any other ministers from appearing when Margaret
Thatcher took to the airwaves so there was never any chance
of a Cabinet member appearing to diverge from her line.
When I was editor of *Today* in the 1990s, the party spin operations were in overdrive, and New Labour was particularly
ruthless about pushing its story of the day, with threats of
retribution if editors disagreed. More than once, I arrived in
the office to find producers in distress – even in tears – because of tongue-lashings from communications officers. So,
there has been no time when things worked perfectly.

But politicians would typically do only one or two interviews each morning. For many years, *BBC Breakfast*
disdained routine political encounters and left all the politicians to *Today*. LBC wasn't a player either. Now, even the
BBC's Sunday morning flagship has to witness its guests
interviewed first on the rival show on Sky News. At its
most industrialised, interviewees can additionally sit in
a small studio in London and be connected to BBC local

radio stations across the country – each with their own five-minute slots with the supposed newsmaker. I have done this myself in my BBC Sport days, and it is seriously disorientating being asked the same thing time after time and having to remember whether you're speaking to Cumbria or Kent.

So, I have sympathy with the politicians who are conveyed from outlet to outlet, trying to remember 'the line to take' that they've been given by government or party officials. I have even more sympathy with interviewers who know exactly what the politician is going to say – because they've already said it three times elsewhere – but who also have to deliver something fresh to their audience. That is why, I'm sure, interviewers sometimes interrupt too early. They've heard the spiel, they know the line that's coming, so they cut it off and try to get something fresh.

One way of getting round this is to ask an unexpected question. This can be an attempt at a 'gotcha!' revelation. One of the early examples was during my controllership of 5 Live when the Labour school standards minister Stephen Byers had called for children to learn their times tables off by heart. Presenter Eleanor Oldroyd asked him on air what the answer was to eight times seven – and he replied: 'Fifty-four.' There was much chortling throughout the land, especially from people who knew that the answer is fifty-six, but it was a completely legitimate question in the circumstances. If he hadn't been talking about arithmetic, it would have been less so. Also fair: I liked the attempt by Andrew Marr to clarify Keir Starmer's personal politics when he asked him at the 2021 Labour conference whether people who thought only women have cervixes were welcome in the Labour Party. But it then lost its uniqueness when every news programme threw in a question about anatomy and gender to Labour interviewees for the next three days.

They did so because a curveball question has at least some chance of breaking down the over-briefed robotic interviewees. It's a case of 'please give me an answer that's vaguely interesting' and an unspoken 'even better if it makes page 3 of the *Daily Telegraph*'.

The apparent ubiquity of politicians is particularly the case with party leaders who will give short-pooled interviews to reporters when they are out and about, so it is a rare day when the bulletins don't have a short clip available of the PM or the Leader of the Opposition. These are almost never from proper sit-down interviews; they are 'news hits' on the day, in which the shouty people from the Downing Street press corps finally get round to asking a sensible question and the politician agrees to give a reply. It was therefore difficult to argue that Johnson or Starmer were hiding from the media, but Johnson was conspicuously evasive about anything that involved long-form scrutiny of his views. He has always loved stunts and photo opportunities and quick soundbites but does not love sitting down to be grilled for an hour.

This may be because of his experience with Eddie Mair back in 2013, when Mair was sitting in for Andrew Marr on the BBC. The encounter is even more revealing now than it was then. Mair asked Johnson, at the time a popular Mayor of London and national 'character', why he had made up a quote when working on *The Times* for which he was sacked. Why, also, had he told a 'bare-faced lie' to his party leader Michael Howard about an affair when he was an MP? And why in his early life had he appeared to condone violence against someone targeted by his friend? Mair's punchline was brutal: 'You're a nasty piece of work, aren't you?' I watched it live, and I was taken aback by that phrase. It is a rare thing for an interviewer to say to a senior politician, and I wondered how justified it was, even though there was the supporting evidence. But now it seems a completely legitimate challenge and one which wasn't applied enough during Johnson's rise. Character matters as well as policy, and the fact is that neither were scrutinised enough. The 'Boris' character was allowed to sail on, with all the consequences for him and for us.

It is certain that the mechanics of interviewing is a subject where the public care less than the media. The 2019 election campaign had a flurry about Johnson refusing to take part in the Andrew Neil interviews, in which Neil had already brilliantly dissected Nicola Sturgeon and Jeremy Corbyn. (It is an example of where a nailed-down version of the grid, with a commitment from the start that Johnson would appear, would have helped.) The media were duly scandalised, and Neil delivered an admonitory monologue to the Prime Minister: 'The theme running through our questions', he told viewers, 'is trust – and why at so many times in his career, in politics and journalism, critics and sometimes even those close to him have deemed him to be untrustworthy.'

It could have been Mair revisited, which is one reason why the interview didn't happen. But there was no dent in Johnson's poll ratings – and unless I missed it no real attempt by the broadcasters to follow up with a concerted take on that theme of trust. Johnson was allowed to chug around the country for photo opportunities in which he knocked down walls labelled 'Brexit', and there was little scrutiny of his character. That was until it was revealed he'd had all those parties in Downing Street, when broadcasters talked incessantly about his character and concluded he'd been a bad 'un all along. There were similar omissions during the leadership of Jeremy Corbyn: was he really up to being Prime Minister? Those who watched him close up thought emphatically not. Perhaps the outcome of negative report cards for both party leaders was just too depressing to share.

What might have stood us in better stead was more vigorous analysis of Johnson and Corbyn before they led their parties. If they had faced the modern equivalent of Robin Day or Brian Walden for an hour of peak-time television every now and again, would they have got away with it in quite the way they did? The public might have formed a view and decided that they did care, and so might electors in the two major parties. When they were in office, neither Johnson (as Foreign Secretary and as party leader) nor Corbyn were even regulars on the *Today* programme. Our greatest exposure to them was during campaigns when the same soundbites were repeated over and over again.

So, my proposals are simple. Cherish the great interviewers. Give them not just the regular platforms – *Today*, *Channel 4 News*, *Newsnight* – but extra ones too. Paxman's Iraq interview with Blair was a special programme for peak-time BBC Two, watched by more than 4 million people. Don't worry about dropping an edition of *DIY SOS*: this is actually more important for broadcasting and the public. And do not lose faith in the power of the airwaves to hold politicians to account.

CHAPTER 16

BIN THE CLICHÉS

Broadcast news is a daily wonder in its delivery of information under extreme time pressure, and also in how journalists grapple with boundless digital capacity. I was lucky to come from a better-resourced generation which had less airtime to fill and therefore more time to think – and, crucially, the opportunity to fail. If a piece wasn't working, we could chuck it in the bin. That's much harder when budgets are tighter, there's nobody spare on the rota and somebody is wondering if you can do live pieces on the hour every hour for multiple platforms. Oh, and there's a request for 500 words on the website about what this all means.

It is therefore unavoidable that some shortcuts are made and that broadcasting clichés abound. You will have plenty of your own to add, and I plead guilty to past and present cliché sins.

The first is the fetishising of 'liveness', which can make the job of a reporter in the field more difficult. There are two kinds of live reporting. One is brilliant on-the-spot broad-casting of the kind we saw during the invasion of Ukraine, and in the evacuation of Afghanistan when brave journalists were in the middle of throngs of people and conveying the heat and the dust and the despair of Kabul. The other is the rather less compelling live contribution which is an editor's attempt to jazz up a dull bulletin. Reporters are sent out to discover what's happening and talk to locals, but too often they find themselves standing next to the satellite truck chattering away to the rolling news services. It wouldn't matter so much if they had anything new to say, but many times they don't. A story has happened, the facts haven't changed – but the studio anchor is still keen to go over to the location for 'the latest'. In a worst case, the latest is what's being fed into the reporter's earpiece by the studio in London where they're reading the agency reports based on sources the reporter hasn't had time to speak to.

This becomes more curious when all that matters, really, is the location; there isn't even any basic newsgathering. The prime example is royal stories. 'We go over now to our royal correspondent, who is outside Buckingham Palace' – where we can be absolutely certain that the Queen did not swing by just before the broadcast to give a briefing. Throughout Prince Andrew's turbulent times, reporters have been stationed outside Windsor Castle – where he doesn't live – to relay thoughts based on stories developing in New York and London. But the castle does look pretty by night.

The recent director of BBC News Fran Unsworth used to talk about what she called 'we name the guilty building' syndrome, which was the stationing of reporters outside a government department or Scotland Yard or a bank or wherever a scandal had broken. The nameplate would be there in view, but the prime actors were nowhere to be seen – and by ten at night they might well be at home watching a reporter outside their office offering an opinion on what they had done or what they might be thinking.

It would be a more persuasive format if the reports gave a unique insight into an issue, but they usually don't. A former television editor sums it up:

> If we must have templates, how about some new ones? What is the point of pieces to camera with no new information or meaningful background location? How long will the public put up with reporters being sent to a site only to stand there and repeat information available elsewhere – their presence in the location having no role in what they know about the story. I increasingly feel, on hearing a cue, that I could deliver the report myself, even if I know nothing about the story apart from what I've heard earlier.

There is a special variety of the contagion boosted by what we might call 'preview-itis'. This is where a correspondent is deployed to somewhere something might happen later on in the day. They speculate about what that something could be, and we usually end up none the wiser for their dawn journey. Not that preview-itis is confined to breakfast programmes. The amount of speculation about what might be in the Sue Gray report reached epic proportions. 'Our political correspondent looks at what the long-anticipated report is likely to find when it appears' was a typical website headline, cheerfully ignoring the fact that our political correspondent didn't have a clue.

Then there are the over-familiar tropes of the packaged reports. If there is a tragedy somewhere, the community is always 'close-knit'. Murders never happen in places where nobody knows their neighbours. Priests, usually invisible in television reporting, appear to reassure us that the community is coming together in times of trouble, and people are televised at Sunday services, which the vast majority in the locality would never attend. At the end of the report, we are often told that the question on everyone's mind is, 'How could this happen here?' Or there is a demand, for instance from a reporter standing in floodwater, that 'there must be answers', even if an average viewer would conclude that rivers sometimes overflow and homes nearby get flooded.

I have been responsible for countless pieces which have done this kind of thing, and it is inevitable that reporters under pressure of time will hit the function key for 'local tragedy' and the clichés will roll. But there are mitigations and improvements that are possible. One is to put a premium on good writing, and especially on television writing to pictures. There are still plenty of people who can do it. On a recent judging panel, I was impressed by the BBC's South Asia correspondent Yogita Limaye; CNN's Clarissa Ward and Nima Elbagir; Stuart Ramsay from Sky News; and ITN's Robert Moore and John Irvine. The fact the first three are all younger confirms that you don't need to be an old-timer to write properly. For their best stories, the common factor was that they had been given time to get out and report and had not had their feet glued to a satellite point. Many Washington correspondents were doing live updates from their bureaux as the Capitol was stormed on 6 January 2021, whereas Robert Moore went to the building and filmed what was happening. The craft was in turning that chaos into a scintillating piece of television for 10 p.m. In other words, value reporters for their reporting and not their ability to fill hours of news channel airtime.

They need brilliant camera operators and location producers too, but producers have a further obligation. One battle-seasoned veteran explains: 'On-air talent are allowed to develop maddening habits and poor broadcasting techniques. It used to be part of an editor's or producer's job to catch these and deal with them. It is too often apparent now that is no longer done or even seen as a duty.'

She is right. I have never for one moment wanted to move back into broadcasting, but I still have the occasional twitch in my armchair when I see excellent reporters using a sloppy script line or fluffing their delivery in a way that could easily be put right. This seems to have become worse in the latest resurgence of multi-platform working, so the expertise of a radio or television specialist is eroded by the urge to produce more stuff that can be used everywhere. Hugh Sykes, a classic example of a brilliant radio reporter, underlined this in a recent conversation:

> Reports can now be just copies of the TV audio, not even re-versioned for radio. Reporter links often 'jump' audibly to the reporter's piece-to-camera, which works in vision but is jarring and confusing on the radio. Also the quality of the TV sound is often a lot worse than the standards required for clarity on the radio.

This matters because you know quality when you see and hear it. And if it's not the well-funded broadcasters who are producing it, then who is? But this is not just about craft skills and the better use of language or the avoidance of mindless blather; it is also about the originality of thought that goes into the commissioning of pieces and deciding what makes it into the headlines. Sometimes there isn't enough.

CHAPTER 17

BE CLEVERER

I was chatting on the phone one evening to a television news producer and we talked about the media reporting of universities – which, having worked at a university for nine years and got to know how they operate, I find rather lame. He agreed. He cited a piece that was running on the day of our conversation about a strike by the University and College Union (UCU) in protest at pay and conditions, including the higher education pension scheme. 'The report gets nowhere,' he said. 'There's a clip of the union saying everything's terrible. There's a soundbite from a Vice-Chancellor arguing they can't afford to pay any more. And there are some vox pops with students who don't want their education to be disrupted but sympathise with their lecturers.' It was rather like a greengrocer warning you that his apples taste like cardboard. I hadn't seen the report at that point, but when I caught it on a bulletin later it was just as feeble as he'd described. University strike covered, yes. But no viewer would be any the wiser about the issues at stake.

This is not saying that there is one version of the truth to be found here. Rather, let me give you some options. The university pensions scheme, the USS, is probably the most troubled in the UK. It has a massive deficit and has been trying to restructure for years. So, the unions are right that the level of payments is becoming onerous, with benefits being reduced, while the employers are also correct about the financial burden on them which might in turn diminish their teaching and research. How has this happened? What is the way out? There are pensions and finance experts readily available, so it might have been a good idea to ask them. Higher-education specialists exist too.

If you fancy something more political, there are two other possible questions. Has the UCU become harder line and more militant? Journalists in the past have interrogated the motives of the radical left in the train drivers' unions or further back the miners – so has that now become a stronger factor in the middle-class educational unions, reflecting the demographic shifts in politics? The employers, who are not exactly a bunch of fire-breathing right-wingers, fume about the intransigence of the UCU's leadership. If that's not your cup of picket-line tea, how about examining the Vice-Chancellors instead? Much of the anger in the unions reflects the widening gap between the top executives in the universities and the average lecturers. Vice-Chancellors, including the one in Cambridge, can be on close to £400,000 a year, so given that is accompanied by a tottering pension scheme and demoralised staff, how can they possibly be worth it?

Most important of all is the student experience. This is rarely portrayed in a way that I recognise. (I should say that I live on the same site as 700 of them.) Early in the pandemic, students were seen locked in tower blocks patrolled by security guards. This, a thankfully rare occurrence, became an image of universities in lockdown. More comically, a later piece looked at the continuing closure of universities by government order – and included interviews with students who were on campus. Nobody seems to have thought to ask why they were there if the universities were closed, and in fact more than half of all students were in residence despite the national shutdown because of the range of exemptions that were permitted. I thought that was quite an interesting phenomenon which affected hundreds of thousands of people. When reporting the subsequent strike, it would have been a good opportunity to look at how the pandemic and industrial action had come together: what evidence was there of any cumulative damage to their learning, and why couldn't the employers and the union have had their row at a less critical moment?

I can hear the voice of a hard-pressed reporter or desk producer saying: 'We haven't got time to do a current affairs piece for every item,' and it is true that a more detailed examination of these issues might be better done in a longer-form programme. But there is always the opportunity to ask an expert to help make a story better. I spoke to my Selwyn College colleague Professor Grant Stewart, a cancer surgeon, about some of the medical stories he sees in the media, and his views chime with those of many other doctors: 'A lot of good stuff in medical research doesn't make it into the mainstream media,' he says.

> Whereas I sometimes look at items on a news website and think: 'There isn't any kind of story there,' and at worst it can be complete twaddle. There is a particular kind of item which bears the imprint of an over-eager press office or an academic seeking a new grant, and what's described as a 'breakthrough' often is something that's only incremental. It may not even come from someone who is well respected in their own field.

So, it's about seeking the right advice – and then also about making the connections between the stories, and especially the ones that shape our lives. That was a view expressed decades ago by John Birt, while he was at London Weekend Television. He wrote in *The Times* in 1975:

> Our economic problems, for instance, manifest themselves in a wide variety of symptoms – deteriorating balance of payments, a sinking pound, rising unemployment, accelerating inflation and so on. The news, devoting two

minutes on successive nights to the latest unemployment figures or the state of the stock market, with no time to put the story in context, gives the viewer no sense of how any of these problems relate to each other. It is more likely to leave him confused and uneasy ... Feature journalism tends to focus on one aspect or one instance of a major problem rather than on that problem as a whole ... For example, making a film about homeless people is not an adequate way of approaching the problems created by our housing shortage.

Well, apart from the quaint gendered language – I'd say that's bang on. How often do we see people complaining about the cost-of-living crisis, but without an explanation of the macroeconomic forces at play? The perpetual prism of politics means that it's often presented as the actions of a couple of people – the Prime Minister and the Chancellor – acting within a Westminster context that then affects people shopping on the high street. A rebel Tory backbencher, bothered about the price of gas, can be portrayed as a more important player than the central bankers or constrictions in the supply chain from China.

Birt was correct, too, in that point about social issues. A flagship bulletin recently ran a piece about a jobless family's poverty very close to an item about record numbers of job vacancies, apparently without identifying even a fleeting connection or seeking to explain it. I have seen countless moving films about people out on the streets on freezing nights or about families living in terrible conditions, but almost none make a link with the national shortage of affordable housing and the debate about reforming planning laws. A former colleague remembers calling a regional television planning desk to offer them a story about a local council being one of the first in the country to resume the construction of council houses. 'We'll get back to you,' said the producer, 'but to be honest it does sound a bit boring.' It can tug at the heartstrings to see the plight of individuals – candidly, it makes good TV – but it seems to be too onerous to examine how they might best be helped.

Remember the quote from Helen Boaden earlier, when she spoke about the media's demands for 'black-and-white answers to overwhelmingly complicated problems'? And I would add the wise observation of another former colleague, George Entwistle, who used to like to point to the complexity of issues raised at *Newsnight* editorial meetings. He told me:

My feeling was that *Newsnight*'s job at the end of the evening was to reintroduce all the subtlety and complexity that arguments and issues inevitably lost during two-minute news packages. It was intended as a politically impartial injunction: straight left- and right-wing takes were both, always, an insult to one's intelligence. Hence I used to say: 'It's more complicated than that.'

Compare and contrast the amount of coverage given to the A-Level algorithm fiasco in the summer of 2020 – and the number of interviews with tearful students and angry parents – with the complete lack of interest in the principle of A-Levels and whether specialism at sixteen is a good idea. *The Times*'s Education Commission, a welcome exception, produced some insightful recommendations about how to reform schools and help the economy, but I can't recall any concerted attempt to do the same on television. Too difficult, again, and easier to send Sue Perkins on a camper-van tour of America?

Smarter commissioning can mean being more imaginative, too, in the choice of stories. Of the many things I am guilty of myself, an over-obsession with America was one – and it lingers in the present day. This has multiple manifestations. The most shameful ones are when terrible weather events rip across the Caribbean and leave scores of people dead, but the live television coverage only really gets underway when the storm hits Florida and a CNN reporter has to battle to stand upright in the wind and rain. All extreme weather events in the United States are automatically deemed to be of interest to British viewers, so a heavy snowfall in New York City will make a nice picture story while storms in Spain evoke not much interest at all.

It is even worse in politics. For years BBC managers vowed to downscale coverage of the Iowa caucuses and the New Hampshire primary and the nominating conventions, despite the excitement of correspondents who wanted to cover every moment of the American presidential process. And I love that stuff myself: I eagerly consumed Theodore H. White's books about the making of different Presidents, which had every bit of political drama you could want in the 1960s and 1970s. But now? The conventions in particular are confections cooked up for American television, and British channels could easily give them a miss.

Meanwhile, in Europe the contest for a successor to Angela Merkel was barely covered. I can imagine the laughter if a junior sub-editor suggested doing an explainer about the CDU–CSU nomination system for the German Chancellorship, even if it is a simpler process than an American caucus. I was in a panel discussion on LBC on the night that the new German partnership between the SPD, the Greens and the Free Democrats was formed, and a caller asked why the British media was taking so little interest in it. It's hard to avoid the conclusion that editors just don't care enough, even though the actions of the German coalition – in our continuing relationship with the EU and the foreign policy response to Ukraine – do affect every British life.

More insidiously, extremes attract. Again, think about how many stories you heard about the rise of the AfD – the far-right Alternative für Deutschland Party – versus the tepid interest in the surge of the German Greens. And how many overviews have there been about why European politics is fragmenting or the collapse of social democracy?

(The Labour Party in the UK is doing well, relatively.) I read about this in the newspapers and current affairs magazines, so it's legitimate to ask why it is so scantily covered by broadcasters.

There is some connection, I would say, with the decline of the 'second package' on television news, especially on the BBC's ten o'clock bulletin. This meant, at its simplest, a packaged report saying what had happened, followed by a second piece trying to explain why. One of its most illustrious former editors Kevin Bakhurst explains:

> The tendency on routine news days has become to try to squeeze some analysis into a single report that tells the story of the day, so a correspondent will give reaction and then context, analysis and explanation all in one. In my view that risks short-changing every part of that. For me the second package can give carefully crafted and well-thought-through analysis, and it allowed the telling of the on-the-day news story the space for the narrative and room to breathe. We used the brilliant specialist correspondents – the people that BBC journalism is built on – and asked them to explore alternative views and voices in their analysis.

I concur. Too often now the first and only package is followed by a short interview featuring the same correspondent, who will say much the same thing again in an unstructured personal take. Bakhurst recalls the way the second packages could add to the programme's impact:

> Some of them that I can remember were from people like Evan Davis, James Robbins and Jeremy Bowen, which asked: why does that story matter? Why should we care? What does it mean for us/the UK/the world? They often challenged the accepted narrative and included clips from big thinkers (former ambassadors or chief executives, say). On themes like the explosion of credit in the UK; on the diplomatic response to Darfur; on the capture of Saddam [Hussein]; or the Arab Spring. The trick really was to be interesting, engaging and accessible enough for a big general audience, while telling experts or even protagonists watching the *Ten* something they didn't know.

Of course, I like the point about 'challenging the accepted narrative'. When I look back on the pieces I oversaw, especially on the *Today* programme, it is the counterintuitive ones of which I'm most proud. My deputy editor on the programme, Rod Liddle, gives an account of the genesis of one item:

> There was a remarkable scene in one BBC *Today* programme morning meeting in about 1995 as the producers gathered together to discuss what stories would be on the following day's show.

The big story was the European Union; the splits occasioned by the EU within the Tory Party and the battle, on the part of racist neanderthal xenophobes, to keep us out of the Exchange Rate Mechanism, from which we had ignominiously exited three years before. The meeting cackled and hooted at the likes of Bill Cash and his assorted fascists on the Eurosceptic right. 'They think the Germans are determined to dominate Europe!' ... How everyone laughed. And then a voice suddenly cut through this jubilant unanimity. 'What if they're right?'

Problem was, in this particular morning meeting, the voice of questioning dissent came from the programme's then editor, Roger Mosey. So the producers suddenly had to entertain the possibility, for the first time, that there might be a shred, an iota, of substance in the Eurosceptic arguments.

Rod overeggs it about the *Today* producers, who were a good bunch, and it would be hard to portray me as a defender of Bill Cash. More soberly, what resulted from that editorial discussion was a splendid piece the following morning about the German strategic approach to Europe – not in the absurd tabloid sense of Berlin wishing to create the German empires again but how Germany seeks to maximise its influence in the EU. It was balanced and impartial, and it added to understanding. Similarly on *Today* I oversaw a series on poverty and how it might be alleviated – but we also included reports on alleged 'fecklessness': the people who, no matter what help they received, could never get their lives together. How much should ordinary working people support out-of-the-ordinary non-working citizens who really did go to the pub to spend the child benefit? Some people are terrible parents. These are thoughts that voters have more often than media producers. In television, society is frequently portrayed as being at fault, whereas in many communities of the UK a belief in individual responsibility remains powerful.

Journalism should never be afraid to tackle tough issues, and it is improved by not accepting things at face value. There are plenty of traps to fall into on everyday stories. For instance, authorities aren't always wrong and self-defined victims of their decisions aren't always right; some decisions are conscientiously taken. Non-disclosure agreements are a bad thing if they shut down whistleblowers, but there are times when a confidentiality pact can be in the interests of both parties in resolving a dispute. Claiming expenses fraudulently is a crime, but putting in the receipts for legitimate expenditure is fine. I remember a poor panellist on *Question Time* who was booed when he revealed that the BBC had paid for his train fare to a distant location. What was he supposed to do? Hitchhike?

I have tried to avoid urging greater 'cleverness' up to now, because it sounds too much like the rewarding of children with neatly polished shoes at a school prize-giving. But I do believe, certainly, that we should nurture and cherish intelligence in daily journalism, because that is what our society needs and what many news-hungry viewers expect. Some are content to sit in a comfort zone, and social media is adept at providing that. But the best news programmes will add a notch or two to the level of challenge – and yes, sometimes provoke. Long may they do so.

CHAPTER 18

RIDE THE PLATFORMS

A milestone was reached early in 2022. The BBC News Instagram account passed 20 million followers, confirming it as the biggest news account on the platform worldwide. It has since risen further. Instagram, often associated with loving pictures of your dinner, is a solid source of news too. CNN is not far behind the BBC, and the *New York Times* is also into eight figures. Meanwhile TikTok, a platform beloved of younger relatives and university students, is also featuring news content. Sky News has more than a million followers there.

This is good. What it represents is mainstream news brands distributing their content as widely as they can, and it is much healthier if social media users are coming to organisations which have a commitment to truth rather than listening only to crazed conspiracy theorists in Kentucky. This is overwhelmingly about younger audiences, too: the

BBC reckons its Instagram account reaches mainly people in their early to mid-twenties.

What is also encouraging is that the main providers are debating whether being on these new platforms leads to a dumbing down of their content, and they are coming to the correct conclusion in my view: it shouldn't.

Martha Holeyman, assistant digital editor at Sky News, tackled the issue in an interview with *Press Gazette*, noting that it is 'explainer' content that is working well across all platforms:

> From the pandemic it's been clear that everyone's looking for everything to be explained a lot more and at a higher frequency as well, because there are so many questions every single day ... probably another secret to the TikTok success is that it's a short-form video form of explaining really.
>
> We don't want to try to be something that we're not in the content that we're creating ... We are using our main top correspondents from Sky News, but not dumbing down the content. We're not approaching the types of stories that we do trying to focus on light news – our top-performing stories are to do with Covid, they're to do with politics, they're to do with the Russia–Ukraine conflict and it's just basically proving that that audience is there.

The BBC was initially wary about TikTok, but the war in

Ukraine revealed the audience need and the corporation took to TikTok in English and Russian. Digital director Naja Nielsen explained to journalism.co.uk: 'We could have launched earlier, but to me, it was just important that we knew that it was well-resourced when we did it.'

It is true that every platform and every format consumes time, effort and money, and the scale of the cutbacks at BBC News means there has to be prioritisation. But all the main broadcasters should steam ahead with getting as much of their core content onto as many platforms as possible – so long, crucially, as it doesn't tip the balance within news-rooms towards entertainment and amusing animal stories. I have watched some Sky News videos on TikTok and they avoid that trap, with some genuinely interesting content.

There is more than an echo here from the 2012 Olympics. From that breathtaking moment in Singapore in 2005, when London won the right to host the Games, my colleague in BBC Sport Dave Gordon – who knows more about Olympic broadcasting than almost anyone else alive – had a gleam in his eye. The explosion of digital technology meant this would be an opportunity to deliver more content on more platforms than ever before. It was as recently as Sydney in 2000 that the BBC had only its two terrestrial channels to cover the Games, backed by the fledgling BBC Sport web-site, which was overwhelmingly text-based. By the time of Athens in 2004 there was the first of the red-button servic-es, and that had grown to six channels for Beijing in 2008.

But for London we wanted to give audiences live access to every event from the beginning to the end of each session, and there was a meeting – a combination of excitement and trepidation – when we concluded that this would mean creating twenty-four extra channels for the duration of the Games. If 10 million people were watching the athletics on BBC One, there would still be demand, we believed, from tens of thousands of people for weightlifting on BBC Olympics channel No. 17.

So, when journalists asked us which was more important, our digital offering or the conventional TV channels, the answer, greedily, was 'both'. It is possible to innovate technologically and also excel in your more conventional offerings. We knew that for London 2012 the biggest audiences would be on BBC One, and a terrestrial channel would be the place where most people followed the pick of the action for the majority of the time. Originally, we had envisaged the twenty-four extra channels being online with some of them available via the red button, but then there was a deal done with Sky to turn the streams into proper television channels. I recall walking through the Olympic broadcasting centre a few nights before the opening ceremony and seeing a television gallery in which all our channels were being tested. I was too nervous to acquire a warm glow from all those screens – there was too much at that point that might go wrong – but with the safety of hindsight it's a matter of pride for our whole team that we launched more channels than at any time in the BBC's history. Even if it was only for seventeen days.

This was only part of the digital innovation. We offered catch-up services on our website and a multiplicity of clips and highlight reels, though at the time the mobile phone network wasn't mature enough to deliver everything we wanted in video. But we did everything we possibly could, and the audience reaction was beyond our expectations both in numbers and in enthusiasm. We watched the statistics each day and monitored the audience comments, though the anecdotal evidence was useful too. I went into a shop in the Olympic Park and heard an assistant chatting about the virtues of the BBC coverage. He'd been watching one event on BBC One and another on his iPad, and he'd been tweeting to his friends about British gold medals. In this one person there was the delivery of our pledge to 'never miss a moment'.

There were two things I'd single out as enabling this to happen. The first was that we were allocated money – not money beyond our wildest imaginings but the proper resources to deliver something special for the entire country. The second is that the BBC's digital teams and technologists were engaged right from the start; it was something about which they cared passionately. This isn't always the case, for perfectly understandable reasons: every programme wants a website and a gizmo and some clever application that they've seen elsewhere, and there just isn't the staffing or the money to make it happen. But nobody doubted that the Olympics was a showcase for the BBC and for Britain, with an overt commitment that broadcasting would change. 1936 was the breakthrough moment for radio, when the nation gathered to hear about the abdication of Edward VIII. The happier event of the coronation in 1953 defined the arrival of television. We wanted 2012 to achieve the same for digital media, and I think it just about did.

Crucially, it was never about creating different content or attempting to be 'down with the kids'. It was recognisably the same BBC Sport which produced London 2012 as the organisation which had delivered London 1948 – transformed by technology but infused by the same values. We celebrated the pioneers who had covered those Games in post-war austerity and who seized the opportunities of their times, as we did of ours.

Which brings us to News in the present day – and its chance to do something similar. The major public service news brands have shown encouraging signs that they can live and thrive in the digital maelstrom. But they do that best when they are themselves, with the brand values which attract audiences to their conventional TV channels. There has been a splendid example of that with Ros Atkins's videos for the BBC, which were originally designed for the relatively low-audience continuous television channels. They gave time – often seven or eight minutes – to explaining stories in depth, and they had the kind of analysis that I used to like in the second packages on the bulletins. And yet they have also done great business online, becoming viral hits and getting millions of views for each piece. A BBC insider whispered to me that this disproved some of the conventional thinking of the social media teams that short videos and quick clips are what cut through, but the lesson is that a clever and structured item can make it too. And that is perfectly logical: the public broadcasters can offer pieces that nobody else can – so there is no need to do what everybody else is doing. It's a rare case of a win-win: grab hold of the digital opportunities and enhance your reputation too.

CHAPTER 19

AND FINALLY (ALMOST): SPORT

I had the happy experience with BBC Radio 5 Live of being its controller in the 1990s and also a soppily devoted fan of radio sport. It used to be the only way of following many live events, especially when football disappeared behind a paywall, and it was indispensable for knowing how your team was getting on and keeping in touch with the sporting gossip. But I doubt that there are many people now who only know the scores and the headlines through 5 Live. Social media and official club channels can offer a more targeted, faster service, and coverage of sport has ballooned across multiple television channels in a way that means, if you're able to afford the subscriptions, you can experience every key moment. The changing expectations of audiences were why, in my later period as the BBC's director of sport, we abolished *Grandstand* and opted instead for prioritising live events and round-the-clock sports information. At the time it felt like we'd slaughtered Bambi, live after the end of indoor bowls from Great Yarmouth, but I've never had any doubt that it was the right thing to do. The worst option would have been a continuing decline into irrelevance.

Yet echoes of that age can still be heard. Every Saturday night on the BBC One late news, we still go through the rigmarole of: 'If you don't want to know the scores, look away now' – as if we were still in the age of *The Likely Lads* and the wonderful episode about Bob and Terry trying to avoid knowing the result of the big match. It's done, of course, to protect the sensibilities of *Match of the Day*, which follows in the schedule and likes to pretend that we have been locked in a shed all day and come to the programme with zero knowledge of what's happened. But the question isn't about whether we need the warning; it's much more about whether television bulletins need the traditional sports desks at all. If you want to know what happened in the big games, you'll most likely have seen everything already.

This is emphatically not about chopping sport from news programmes. Rather, it is the belief that sports news, like the rest of the output, can become more ambitious in its purpose. It should be less about groin strains, more about the business of sport and the way it affects our lives.

I spoke to David Kogan, a former senior journalist and executive and more recently the man behind the Premier League's astonishing rights deals which brought billions into the English game. 'News editors and producers tend to relegate sport against other subjects, which is quite wrong,' he said.

Three reasons. First, people really care about sport and that makes it news. Second, it produces huge stories. Look at the announcement of the European Super League and the way that clubs and fans became entangled with regulators and national governments and the EU. Third, the economics and technology of sport matter. There is more money spent on sport than anything else in broadcasting. It's a huge business story, and it also drives massively the technology of broadcasting and everything we consume in the media.

Another former colleague, Dominic Coles, was my right-hand man in BBC Sport and the negotiator who secured the Olympics – including London 2012 – for the BBC. He agrees: 'With the arrival of the private equity firms, sovereign nations and (often) bored billionaires, sport is destined to get even bigger'. Coles underlines the strategic importance of this to public service broadcasting:

Sport is as important to the nation as ever. The power of sport is that it doesn't get hemmed in by regional boundaries or class or ethnicity, and it is truly international, national, regional and local. If the likes of the BBC and ITV really want to remain meaningful, what better way than embracing the importance of sport to their communities?

Examples include the community campaigns to save threatened football clubs. Bury went under, and Derby County's battle for survival is the biggest story in Derby for years. It matters a hundred times more within a news bulletin than a clip of a try from the Betfred Super League.

The broadcasters do get this, though news coverage of sport remains haphazard. One observer is critical of the quality of sports reporting within news bulletins, saying there's too much that's 'average' and without 'curiosity or personality'. At times the volume of sport around big events can be overdone. News bulletins went overboard about British medals in the Tokyo Olympics in a way that became tiresomely repetitive alongside the BBC Sport highlights programmes. Both focused on the same triumphs, and both thought it would be lovely to see how the winners' mums and dads had celebrated the victory with their family and friends. It felt like medallists' parents had moved in to the nations' living rooms. During the London Games we had tried to stop this threat of overkill by delineating the mission more clearly between News and Sport: the former was supposed to give a loftier overview, helped by its location in an East End tower block outside the Olympic Park, while the Sports teams were allowed to be passionate and engaged and right on top of the action. Empowered by the director-general Mark Thompson to be in charge of all the Olympic output, I would chide the BBC News channel for trying to simulcast the live action and tell it to do some journalism instead.

It's not as if the Olympics are ever short of news stories. The Beijing Winter Games shone a spotlight on human rights across China – and for good measure Vladimir Putin dropped by to watch the opening ceremony with Chairman Xi, though he was reported to have fallen asleep during the parade of athletes. In football, the machinations of the awful FIFA led to a World Cup scheduled for early winter in Qatar, with more concerns about human rights. Here at home, we've seen the crisis at Yorkshire Cricket Club as an example of the racism that lingers among the blazered leadership. And every sport has questions about how and why things happen in the way they do, as opposed to just what the result is. Yet it's these themes that can be under-covered – pushed out by the goals from the Champions League which many will have seen earlier, or given no time because political correspondents have been asked yet again to speculate about what might happen next at Westminster. It is good that ITV is extending its evening bulletins, but it remains a squeeze on BBC journalism that the duration of its *News at Ten* has been chopped and changed – usually with the emphasis on chopped – by the schedulers.

Encouragingly, though, there are signs that the corporation's sports journalists are trying to shift the agenda. The BBC's sports editor Dan Roan wrote a piece for the *Radio Times* in 2021, which began by saying how much the world of sport now 'routinely collides with geopolitics, big business, the law and ethics', citing the takeover of Newcastle United by a Saudi-led consortium. He continued:

The actual sport itself – with inspiring tales of drama, triumph and joy – remains fundamental. But so too now is an understanding of the political and financial forces behind sport, and the moral dilemmas it poses. More top athletes are speaking out on a range of social issues and refusing to 'stick to sport'. It has become a medium through which society debates everything from race, gender and food poverty, to sustainability, health and technology.

His piece was pointing to a podcast produced by the BBC called *The Sports Desk*, and it's a decent attempt at digging underneath the headlines. But it will fully succeed if it gets enough of those stories on to the main bulletins and the likes of the *Today* programme. What's more, they should be impartial and critical. Just because a sports star is saying something, it doesn't mean that it's true, and if they want to debate contemporary issues, they should be open to rebuttal like everyone else.

I commissioned two long-form sports news programmes

in my time at the BBC. One, *Sportsweek* on Sunday mornings on 5 Live, ran for more than twenty years and was a success in the way it set the agenda for Monday morning's papers. The other, *Inside Sport* on BBC One, vanished without trace. It is not easy to get past the agents and the sport press officers to get to the prime sources and hear their stories. It is also significantly harder to cover the business of sport than it is to do a sixty-second package on a Test match. But that is no excuse for not trying. Sport is something that engages most of the world and can change it too. It should be moving up the bulletin running orders, not just providing the 'and finally' at the end of the programme.

CHAPTER 20

IT'S UP TO US

So, we have made it to No. 20, and I hope you've found something to agree with along the way. What I think we can say with some certainty is that even in the time I was writing this book the global climate for independent journalism and free speech has become even bleaker. The war by Russia on Ukraine has been accompanied by a crackdown on the remaining independent Russian media outlets, and critics of the Putin regime have been jailed. Day by day, China is eroding the freedoms of Hong Kong and preventing reporters from carrying out their work. It is also ever more apparent that we cannot rely on the giant international media operators to guarantee freedom of expression. The algorithms of the social media giants decide what we can and can't see, with zero accountability. And, as part of a pattern of censorship to please dictatorial regimes, Warner Bros edit out gay references in movies that they want to show in China – or, as they put it in a press statement, make 'nuanced cuts in order to respond sensitively to a variety of in-market factors'.

In response, I trust there is a consensus among fair-minded people that we need public service media to be vigorous and intelligent and focused unerringly on the truth. Its future can best be guaranteed by reinvigorating its traditional values and by embracing the latest technology – while reflecting our vivid, fractured times. We can all play a role in supporting that.

I mentioned that when I set off on my lifetime's journey through broadcasting there was little chance of interaction with the gods of Broadcasting House. In the 1970s, as for the half-century before that, if you felt irritated enough by something, you might write a letter. Or if you wanted to challenge a view expressed on air you might, if you were extremely lucky, make it onto one of the early phone-ins. The name of Radio 4's flagship – *Tuesday Call*, which began in 1973 – reveals how rare the opportunity was. Now we live in a blizzard of interactivity where you would never dream of waiting until next Tuesday. A presenter I know with long experience in radio was taken aback to return to a show after a number of years away and discover major gaps in the running order. 'What do I do there?' he asked. 'Oh, that's for audience interaction' came the reply. 'You just solicit emails and texts and fill with those for a few minutes'. It's similar in some regional news programmes where the views of Harry from Hornsea weigh in alongside the stories of the day.

Some of this is harmless, though it can be tedious and unenlightening too. But far more worrying is the extent to which presenters and producers are exposed to the viciousness of social media while they are performing their duties and the extent to which cyberbullying has become a permanent factor in the lives of many journalists. Even worse are the physical threats and the sense of personal danger that is created. The BBC's Sarah Smith spoke out about this when she left her post as Scotland editor, saying that she had been 'demonised quite heavily amongst certain parts of the population' and that she had encountered 'vitriolic attention' and 'deeply unpleasant' abuse online. The Women in Journalism Scotland group supported her, saying that one of its most requested services was for resilience training for dealing with online abuse: 'We are long overdue a reckoning.' There are countless other examples across the industry and across the UK.

I wonder whether part of the answer is to dial down some of the voluntary interactivity. I was used to a relationship in which a programme would be put out by an editorial team and presenters, and almost nothing would disrupt that relationship. Now, Twitter and the other platforms give a constant commentary on what you're up to, and there's both the dread of an individual piece of abuse and the queasy feeling in your stomach when your programme and your name are trending because of an alleged mistake. On the other side are the presenters who want to trend and spout all sorts of nonsense to make that happen. I therefore increasingly admire the folk who stay away from Twitter, or at least switch it off while they're broadcasting. Their loyalties are, rightly, to the bulk of their audience and not to trolls.

The reason Smith's experience is so concerning is that it is not acceptable in any circumstances, but it also arises simply from doing her job. She is one of the best in the business, seeking to report fairly and accurately and to do all the things that I – and you, I hope – want from our public service broadcasters. What her experience shows is the polarisation in Scottish politics between nationalists and unionists, with sinners on both sides, and which finds its echoes across the UK in the divides between Remainers and Leavers or between the cities and the towns. Unforgivably, one member of the Scottish Parliament initially accused Smith of 'imagining' the abuse, while a former MP said this of her: 'She's never been unbiased … a traitor to the highest metric within journalism. No great loss, as another "cap doffer" shall replace her, and the UK controlled media machine grinds on.'

It matters that we stand firm against this kind of abuse. But it also points to the reason we need to learn from the recent past. The Brexit referendum was a deeply unpleasant experience for many on both sides of the divide, and the toxicity of politics continues. There will be highly contentious issues that we need to face. Another general election is not far away, and there is the possibility of another

Scottish referendum – and maybe even a border poll in Ireland – which will once again put the future of the United Kingdom in the balance. The stakes will be particularly high in Northern Ireland, where the decades of the Troubles gave way to a fragile peace and where violence lurks below the surface on both sides of the sectarian divide. The most important platform for rational debates on all these issues will be public broadcasting; and there will be passion and emotion in future campaigns, as there should be, but there will be facts too. What kind of Ireland would be proposed by the architects of unification and by those who want to keep the north as part of the United Kingdom? In a Scottish independence referendum, the SNP and its allies will need to define their view of Scotland's future. There are multiple challenges. Have they really settled what currency an independent Scotland would use? If they want to rejoin the EU, will they have to commit to the euro? After Russia's nuclear threats to the United Kingdom, does shipping out the Scottish-based deterrent still make sense? And how do they plan to address the kind of trading issues we've seen in Northern Ireland, with possible border checks at Gretna and Berwick? The unionists face the age-old question: why should the nation of Scotland be ruled by a UK government for which it did not vote?

It is right that these questions must be asked, and the policies emerging must be challenged robustly. Even more so, the views of experts must be considered. It would be a dereliction of duty to resort to the robotic balance of the 2016 EU referendum and conclude that 'some people say Scotland will be poorer, while others think it will be better off after independence'.

I am not here being anti-independence. It is the right of the Scottish people to decide their own destiny, as they did in 2014. But my personal judgement on the current facts is that there is a remarkably similar dilemma as with Brexit: if you want to be independent and if nationhood matters more than anything else – then yes, you will vote for that. But if economic stability and a single market between Scotland and England is your goal, then your vote would logically go the other way. What the public broadcasters must do is examine the evidence impartially and then present the facts to the voters, and that is the opposite of what malign individuals on Twitter will want.

What these nation-shaping issues also have in common is that the metropolitan media has been weak in understanding Scottish nationalism in the same way that it was poor at getting the message about Brexit. I don't think it's been great at comprehending Irish nationalism or Ulster unionism, either. I've got this far in the book without using one of my very favourite sayings from the days of editorial meetings, which is that 'two apparently contradictory things can be true'. In this case, for the broadcasters, they have historically been weak in their comprehension of the nationalist tide, but they also now need to be tougher in examining the constitutional and economic implications of splitting the United Kingdom.

At its simplest: you have a better chance of people believing you if you show that you understand them. The London-based media didn't get the UKIP voters of Clacton or the nationalists of Perth, so why should those citizens listen to what the network news says? Preaching to the unconverted – the people not within the metropolitan bubble – may be a tougher thing to do, but it is required both because it is a duty to foster participation in our democracy and because it is a consequence of universal funding.

So, I am certainly not recommending easy options. If our news broadcasting is to be smarter and higher profile and more challenging, it will create more rows. The great upside for the BBC was that it got through the EU referendum without any real aggro, and the downside for the public was that most of its analysis was too anaemic to bother anyone very much. The sweet spot is journalism that is evidenced and impartial but that says something of significance too.

This is where the public, and you and me, matter. We are, I believe, the majority, the 91 per cent of people in recent research who think impartial news is better for society, the people who value accuracy and truth. And we can make our impact in a multiplicity of ways: by watching and listening to the highest quality news programming, by advocating it to our friends and neighbours, by celebrating its successes, by retweeting the BBC and ITN and Sky rather than some wild conspiracy theorist – and yes, by holding such programming to account when it gets things wrong. Not with abusive posts on social media but with reasoned argument and using the accountability processes that all the broadcasters have. We must lobby, too, for our politicians to defend public service – and we can do it with greater conviction if that service is as good as it can be. It is not unreasonable for politicians to be disaffected by broadcasters who misread them or their constituents, but if they see an authentic picture of the modern United Kingdom, they have much less reason to smash the institutions and leave us wading through the marshlands of social media. Ideology-based vandalism should be resisted.

I cannot pretend that this is anything other than in the balance. Political support wavers, funding pressures grow. But the need for high-quality broadcasting is stronger than ever. If Britain throws away the services that bring us together, how would our society function? And if the millions who consume quality news don't speak for it, who will?

AFTERWORD

I will say what's often said at the end of a book: if there's anything you don't like, I accept responsibility. But if you enjoyed what you've read, plenty of other people should take the credit. I am grateful to former colleagues who generously gave their time and shared their views, and most of them are named in the text. Additionally, there are friends who read some of the drafts and told me whether I was barking up the wrong or right tree. In alphabetical order, they include: Catherine Barnard, Dominic Coles, George Entwistle, Simon Heffer, Chris Rybczynski, Sheila Scarlett, Les Sheehan and Eleanor Updale. Additionally, my thanks go to Julie Etchingham, Jeremy Vine and Justin Webb for their fast reading of a close-to-final version and their generous endorsements.

Some sections of the book have had test runs in articles in the *New Statesman* and *The Spectator*, and I appreciate the platforms they and a number of newspapers have given me.

Biteback Publishing was a pleasure to work with – principally Olivia Beattie, editorial director; Lucy Stewardson, my editor; and Suzanne Sangster, publicity director. My agent Alex Armitage gave his customary cheery encouragement, too.

I wrote in the lovely surroundings of Selwyn College, Cambridge. Equally important are the people here: an excellent fellowship and a supportive senior leadership team of Janet O'Sullivan, Mike Sewell and Martin Pierce. The college's students add to the fun of the job and provide appropriate challenge from time to time. I am also encouraged by the number who want careers in the media and are optimistic about what its role can be. It may seem that everything has changed since I first took a job at Pennine Radio in 1979, but in reality a lot is the same too, so I wish the best of luck to people setting out into broadcasting and journalism, and I hope they have as much enjoyment as I did.

INDEX